# POLTERGEISTS
## AND OTHER HAUNTINGS

# POLTERGEISTS
## AND OTHER HAUNTINGS

RUPERT MATTHEWS

ISBN: 978-1-83857-178-8
AD007897UK

Printed in the UK

2 4 6 8 10 9 7 5 3 1

# CONTENTS

# INTRODUCTION

On 29 November 1928 Mr Frederick Robinson was in the kitchen of his modest terraced home in Eland Road, in the London suburb of Battersea, when he heard a strange pattering noise…

It did not sound quite like rain, so Mr Robinson went off to investigate. Looking up through the glass roof of the conservatory, he could see several small pieces of coal, three pennies and a few lumps of soda. As he watched, another tiny bit of coal fell on to one of the glass panels. It rolled down to lodge against a metal beam. Then came silence. Mr Robinson thought that some practical joker was playing tricks on him. When nothing further happened, he went back to the kitchen. Later that day he climbed up a ladder and cleared the roof. After descending, he added the pieces of coal to the family coal scuttle and pocketed the pennies.

On 2 December Mr Robinson heard the noise again. This time he did not bother going into the conservatory. Instead, he rushed towards the garden, hoping to catch the prankster. As soon as he reached the garden, the clatter of small objects stopped. Mr Robinson peered over his back wall but there was nobody in sight. Next day the mysterious shower of objects started again. This time Mr Robinson's nephew, Peter Perkins, was at home. The two men raced into the back garden. Without pausing to look at the conservatory, they vaulted over the back wall, hoping to catch the culprit. There was nobody there. Returning to the garden, the two men were suddenly startled by a terrific crash and the sight of flying glass. When they dashed into the conservatory, they discovered a very large lump of coal had plunged vertically through the glass roof.

That was too much for Mr Robinson. Peter was sent out into the street to find a policeman. This was in the days before working-class families like the Robinsons owned telephones. It was also a time when policemen did not sit in offices, but could be relied upon to be out and about in the community. Peter soon found a policeman, who accompanied him back to the house.

The policeman surveyed the damage, asked questions and made notes. Then he went into the back garden to find out where the coal-thrower might have hidden. Mr Robinson followed while Peter stayed indoors to clear up the mess.

No sooner had Mr Robinson and the constable reached the back garden than an object fell on to the conservatory roof with a tinkle. Peter called out that it was a penny. The policeman looked up just as a second penny came falling down to join the first one. He was baffled. The penny seemed to have fallen straight down from the sky. It would have travelled in an arc if it had been thrown from a neighbouring garden. The officer looked upwards in an attempt to find the source of the falling coin. That was when a large lump of coal hit him forcibly on the back of the helmet. He spun round, but there was nobody there. Then he climbed the back wall, as Mr Robinson had done before him, but again no coal-thrower was to be seen. The policeman was more thorough than Mr Robinson so he spent some time looking about. He even exercised the authority of his uniform by climbing into the neighbouring gardens to search for a likely culprit. He found nothing.

Mr Robinson invited the policeman into the kitchen for a cup of tea. Mrs Robinson put the kettle on, while the three men sat down at the table. The policeman had barely managed to get his notebook out when a large potato hit the table with a thud and rolled towards him. Like the other objects the potato seemed to have fallen directly from above. It would presumably have travelled at an angle if it had been thrown. All three men looked up to see if there was a hole in the ceiling through which a potato could have fallen. They then saw a second potato materialize in mid-air and fall down on to the table. There was a rush to get out of the room. After the policeman had tucked his notebook into his pocket, he said that he was totally baffled and would report the incident to his superiors. Then he left, hurriedly.

The events of December 1928 proved to be the opening salvo of a reign of terror that would afflict the Robinson household for weeks. Furniture would be smashed, ornaments and crockery would dance around the house by themselves and threatening messages would be written on sheets of paper by unseen hands. Unsurprisingly, one member of the family would become so traumatized that he would have to be hospitalized. The police were so baffled that they sent for private investigators. After that the press arrived, along with psychics, mediums and others who professed to be experts in the field of the supernatural. Each new arrival had a novel theory about what was going on and a fresh suggestion for how it should be tackled. Nothing worked and the disturbances continued unabated. Then one day the unexplained events stopped. They never started again and the Robinson household returned to normal.

The Battersea Mystery House, as it became known, had made the headlines across London for weeks. All of the disturbances were thoroughly investigated at the time and they had been witnessed by a range of entirely respectable people, whose testimony must be considered reliable. At various times the events had been annoying, terrifying and spiteful. They remain unexplained.

These days we recognize that the disturbances at Battersea were a poltergeist visitation. All poltergeists are unique, but they share a number of features that make them a distinct phenomenon. In this book I am going to be examining the poltergeist phenomenon. I will be attempting to build up a clear picture of what happens during a visitation and I will be trying to find some answers to the great mystery of the most terrifying and bizarre of all paranormal events.

When all is said and done, the poltergeist is in a league of its own. Witnesses may be open to question, but the material results of a poltergeist visitation are all too real.

*Rupert Matthews*

# chapter 1

# THE OTHER WORLD

The German term 'poltergeist' has been adopted in the English-speaking world. It refers to a particular type of paranormal event. Many other types of inexplicable happenings are witnessed by people from time to time, but they are not recognized by formal science.

The word 'poltergeist' is usually translated as 'noisy ghost', but that does not quite capture the full meaning of the term. The ghost is 'noisy' in much the same way as a party thrown by drunken teenagers is noisy.

Not only is there a large amount of noise, but there is a rumbustious, anarchic degree of movement and jostling that at any moment might turn to violence.

There is also a feeling of potential mayhem about any place that a poltergeist visits. Nor is the 'ghost' part of the translation completely accurate. There is a bit more to it than that.

In German the word might mean a spirit or a disembodied intelligence as often as it might mean a ghost. While some researchers might maintain that a poltergeist visitation is caused by a ghost, others would strongly disagree. It is but one possible explanation among many.

In this book I shall be using the conventional term 'poltergeist' to describe particular phenomena, but I do not wish to imply that I accept the ghostly interpretation. I think that something else is causing the manifestations.

I shall also be using the word 'visitation' to describe the period of time during which a poltergeist is active. Typically a poltergeist visitation has a beginning, a middle and an end. It lasts for a definite period of time, though this can vary considerably, and once it is over it very rarely begins again. I do not mean to imply that the house or the person involved is in fact being visited by some entity that causes the poltergeist activity – that might be the case or it might not. What I do want to say is that just like a visit by an unwanted guest there is, thank goodness, a start and a finish to the career of any given poltergeist you could mention.

Some researchers prefer to use the term 'poltergeist attack', but while some poltergeist events are violent the word 'attack' implies a purpose that might not be there.

## 'Classic Ghosts'

As with any study of the paranormal, it is best to start by setting out what I am seeking to investigate, the categories I am ruling out of the process and how I intend to go about my investigation.

I am most emphatically not attempting to deal with ghosts in the traditional sense of the word. A 'classic ghost', as it is called, is usually a very distinct type of apparition. I have investigated a large number of hauntings of this type and I have spoken to a wide range of witnesses. Take, for instance, the haunting of the Black Horse public house in West Bolden, just outside Sunderland in northern England.

The Black Horse is reputedly haunted by the ghost of a man who was badly wounded during some sort of riot or fracas outside the premises. The unfortunate man was carried into the pub by his friends so that he could receive medical aid, but he died an hour or two later. That happened more than two centuries ago, but the ghost remains. In 2003 the pub acquired a new landlord, who told me about his first encounter with the ghost:

*Well, I was in here opening up one day. Lovely day it was and I had the front door open to let the air in. I was tidying up glasses and stuff by the bar when something made me glance towards the door. That's when I saw this man sitting there by the door looking out the window. He was quite solid, not see-through or anything like that. He was wearing a long dark cloak of a very rough texture. Funny how you remember details. It was coarse and woollen, I felt I could just reach out and touch it. And he had a big dark-coloured hat on with a wide brim. I think he was wearing boots as well, but wouldn't swear to it. He looked about 45 or 50 to me and was pretty heavily built, definitely not a thin man.*

*Anyway, I thought he was an early customer come in to wait for us to open. So I called across, 'Can I help you?', or words to that effect. The man turned to look at me and I suddenly thought how sad he looked. Then he was gone. Just like that. He did not walk off, he did not fade away. Nothing. He was there, then he was gone. I tell you, I left this bar in a real hurry. The hairs on the back of my neck were sticking right up.*

*At first I wasn't sure what to do. I mean, you wouldn't be, would you? I didn't tell anyone what I had seen. Then some time later one of our girls mentioned the pub was meant to be haunted and told me about the man and all. So then I knew that I had seen the ghost. Like I said, I didn't hold with all that when I came here. But I do now.*

Another haunted pub in northern England is the Sun Inn, just north of Houghton-le-Spring, Tyne and Wear. The ghost there is of a middle-aged man, but he has no story to explain his presence. An account of the ghost was given to me by Neil, the chef at the pub:

*Oh right. Well, I've seen him a few times, see. But I got my best look last winter. My washer and me were in here early in the morning doing our prep – you know, getting the vegetables sliced and everything ready for quick cooking. Got to be freshly cooked to taste right, see.*

*Anyhow, we were all alone in the pub and working away when the ghost walks along that corridor out there, past the kitchen door that was open. He was an oldish fellow, I think, and wearing a dark jacket. But you'd know him if you saw him.*

*Haunting figure: the Black Horse Inn near Sunderland is home to a remarkably active ghost, a phantom of the traditional type that would seem to be a very different entity to the poltergeist*

*My mate looks up and says, 'Did you see that? Who was that?' I told him it was just the ghost, but he wouldn't have it. He insisted it was a real person walking around. So we went out into the corridor, but as you can see there is just that door at the end that opens out into the car park at the rear. There was nobody in the corridor, of course, so we open the door and look in the car park. Nobody there. And because it had snowed the night before we could see there were no footprints either. No one had walked out that door and that's a fact. My mate's face was a picture. I reckon he believes in ghosts now all right.*

It is not only buildings that are haunted. Streets and footpaths can be home to ghosts as well. The narrow alleyway known as Royal Oak Passage in the southern English city of Winchester has a ghostly monk.

One witness told me what he gets up to:

*That's right, the monk ghost chap. It was one evening last summer. I'd finished work and was walking back to my car when I cut down that alley by the pub. Nobody else was around at the time. The shoppers had all gone home and the nightlife hadn't got going.*

*Then I saw this figure coming towards me dressed in a long cloak and hood. I thought it was a bit odd because it was a warm evening. Nobody would need to wrap up like that. Then, when we were passing each other, I felt suddenly cold. Like if you stand under the air conditioning unit in a shop.*

*There was this cold draught. I looked round to see what could have caused it, then realized the figure had gone. There was nowhere he could have gone, you see. He was only a couple of feet away from me. Then he was gone.*

There are thousands of these ghosts around the world. The phantom of Abraham Lincoln has been seen in the White House in Washington DC; the spectre of Elvis Presley has been seen wandering around Gracelands, his old home in Memphis, Tennessee; and a 19th-century sailor tramps a narrow street in The Rocks area of Sydney, Australia. What these ghosts have in common is that they are the apparitions of people who are, objectively speaking, no longer there. Witnesses who see these classic ghosts report that during the time that the ghosts are present they appear to be completely solid and normal – they are not semi-transparent as movies and television shows might lead us to expect. The landlord at the Black Horse at West Bolden was at great pains to make this point. He genuinely thought that the ghost was a real person who had come into the pub. He could even recall the texture of the man's coat just as he would have been able to do if he had been looking at a real person.

The chef at the Sun Inn revealed another feature of these ghosts: it is possible to get so accustomed to them that one becomes blasé. Classic ghosts do the same thing time after time. Some stare out of windows while others walk down stairs or stomp along corridors, but whatever an individual ghost might do it always does the same thing each time it is seen. A ghost that sits by a fireside will not suddenly get up and climb a staircase. Nor will a phantom that habitually climbs stairs sit by a fireside. So once you have seen a ghost a couple of times and have become accustomed to what it does, it loses the power to shock or frighten.

Sometimes a noise can be heard when a ghost appears. The ghost of an elderly woman that haunted Hampton Court Palace for some years was accompanied by the sound of a spinning-wheel.

When a spinning-wheel was found bricked up inside a forgotten doorway the ghost and the sound ceased to be encountered. Just as noisy are the ghostly Roman soldiers who march along the route of a former Roman road that is now to be found in the cellar of a house in York. The ghosts tramp along as if greatly dispirited, but they are accompanied by the sound of a high-pitched bugle blast.

Most of these ghosts are attached to a place, such as a house, a pub or a road. A very few of them appear to be attached to an object. A museum in Bridport, Dorset, has a haunted dress, a beautiful 17th-century gown, which was left to the museum. The ghost of a girl walks about in the vicinity of the dress, no matter where it is. She seems to be rather protective of the garment, as if it holds some special memories for her. The apparition does not bother anyone, except for the fact that it appears with startling regularity. The girl used to haunt the house where the dress was formerly kept, but when it was passed to the museum the ghost went as well.

The Corbett Arms Hotel at Market Drayton, Shropshire, has an equally haunted mirror on the first-floor landing. It is a large, gilt-framed mirror that has stood there for as long as anyone can remember. For most of the time it is simply a mirror, which reflects back the images of those that pass by. But just occasionally it will mist over and show the passing guest a totally different view.

The mirror then appears to be reflecting another period in time entirely, because the landing is decorated in another style and people are seen dressed in long gowns and evening wear, or in uniform. The vision lasts only for a second or two, but it can be most unnerving.

Perhaps the best way of understanding such ghosts is to see them as some sort of recording of past events. These phantoms do not normally interact with the witness who sees them, nor do they appear to be capable of moving objects about in any way. They appear to be real, but they do not seem to have a physical reality at all. A great many of these ghosts seem to be connected with events of great emotional trauma, such as broken romances, tragic accidents or sudden deaths. A currently favoured theory has it that human emotions can be imprinted into bricks, stones or landscapes in such a way that the image of the person feeling those emotions can be played back to appear as a ghost when the conditions are right. This idea is generally termed the 'stone tape' theory, though quite how it works is obscure.

## 'Crisis Apparitions'

A quite different type of ghost goes by the name of 'crisis apparition' among investigators. One such apparition was seen on 7 December 1918 at the Royal Air Force base at Scampton, Lincolnshire. A pilot named David McConnell was ordered to fly an aircraft to the RAF base at Tadcaster because it was wanted there the next day. He left at 11.30am, telling his room-mate Lieutenant Larkin that he would return by train and be back in time for supper. At 3.25 that afternoon Larkin sat reading a book in the room he shared with McConnell. He heard footsteps coming up the corridor, the door opened and McConnell stood in the doorway wearing flying kit. His flying helmet was dangling from his left hand.

'Hello, my boy,' said McConnell. This was his usual greeting to Larkin.

'Hello,' replied Larkin. 'You're back early.'

'Yes,' agreed McConnell. 'I had a good trip. Well, cheerio.'

He then shut the door and Larkin heard his footsteps retreating down the corridor. Larkin assumed that his room-mate was going to have tea. Or perhaps he was going to file his flight report.

At 3.45pm another lieutenant, Garner Smith, went to Larkin's room and asked him when McConnell would be back, because they had tickets to a show that evening. Larkin replied that McConnell had already returned, but Smith was convinced he had not. The two men went off to check and discovered that McConnell had not yet reported back, nor had the guard on the front gate seen him arrive. Larkin was adamant that he had seen McConnell, so a search began. The search ended when a telegram arrived from Tadcaster: McConnell's aircraft had crash-landed. McConnell had been badly injured and he had died at 3.25pm – the exact time at which Larkin had seen him arrive back in their room.

Hundreds of similar cases are on file. Most of them are difficult to verify because a phantom is often seen by a person who is alone at the time. There is usually only the word of that single person to rely on. However, the McConnell case is different because of the search made by Smith and Larkin. Dozens of men saw Smith and Larkin walking around the

Scampton base looking for McConnell. Many of them could verify that the search was made long before anyone heard the news of McConnell's death. Although no one, apart from Larkin, saw the apparition, a number of people could testify that he had reported seeing it well before news of the tragedy had arrived.

Another such incident took place in 1926. Miss Godley of County Mayo had gone to visit an elderly man named Robert Bowes, who worked on her estate. He had been forced to take a few days off work due to illness. She took with her the estate steward and a servant named Miss Goldsmith. When Miss Godley saw Bowes she realized that he was seriously ill, so she decided that she would send a boy to fetch the doctor as soon as she got home. As the trio returned home in a pony cart, they were amazed to see Bowes punting a boat across the lake that lay near his home. The boat was about a hundred yards distant, but there could be no mistaking Bowes with his flowing white beard, bowler hat and dark coat. As they all watched, the boat carried Bowes into a reed bed on the far side of the lake and then it vanished from view.

When she got home, Miss Godley followed her earlier plan of sending a boy to the doctor's house. A couple of hours later, the doctor arrived at Miss Godley's house to announce the sad news that Bowes had suffered a sudden seizure and had died about ten minutes after Miss Godley's visit – which was exactly the time at which the phantom Bowes had been seen. This instance is rare in that three different people saw the crisis apparition, instead of the usual one.

Investigators have come up with several ways of explaining how a crisis apparition might come about. One theory is that the person seeing

*Can a mind be read? JG Pratt and Hubert Pearce in the famous ESP tests conducted at Duke University in 1933–4 by JB Rhine, the 'father of modern parapsychology'. The subjects achieved considerable success in communicating the contents of cards*

the apparition has the ability to sense things that are beyond the range of the usual five senses – sight, hearing, smell, touch and taste. This ability is usually called extra-sensory perception, or ESP.

Those who hold this view believe the unconscious mind of the percipient of an apparition knows through ESP that the person in question has died or has suffered some accident. This knowledge is then converted into a visible hallucination by the conscious part of the witness's mind.

According to another hypothesis, when people realize that they are about to die, or suffer a terrible accident, they can somehow send a message to someone to whom they feel closely attached. This ability to send a message directly from one brain to another is called telepathy. The mechanism by which this is achieved is unclear, but it is generally thought to be similar to ESP in some way. A third explanation is that when people are on the point of death they can create an apparition of themselves and project it to a distant place, where it is then seen by whichever witness or witnesses happen to be present. Whether such an apparition is a solid manifestation or an intangible shadow is a moot point. Quite how a person could achieve this by mind power alone is unclear.

No matter which explanation is favoured, the matter is most definitely a paranormal one. Conventional science does not recognize the reality of ESP or telepathy – still less does it endorse stone tapes (the idea that ghosts and hauntings are like psychic 'tape recordings' stored in objects such as rocks to be 'replayed' later) or apparitions projected from a human mind. It would be possible to relate hundreds of accounts of ghosts and apparitions, but none of them have been subjected to close scientific study and there has been no scientific acceptance of the reality of any of the events.

## Studying Poltergeists

A poltergeist is neither a classic ghost nor a crisis apparition. As we shall see in the chapters that follow it is something very different again. However, it does share some features with both of those paranormal events. What classic ghosts, crisis apparitions and poltergeists have in common is the spontaneous and unpredictable nature of their occurrence. One of the key reasons why scientists do not study such phenomena is that it is impossible to take one into a laboratory and look at it. None of these phenomena can be made to perform to order, so unlike chemical reactions or living creatures, they cannot be subjected to tests.

And then there is the danger that a scientist might be subjected to ridicule by his fellows, or be starved of research funds by the authorities, if he should announce that he is investigating ghosts. Similar considerations have held back research into all manner of subjects and topics. No reputable scientist has gone in search of the Yeti or Bigfoot and few have regarded UFOs as a serious topic for investigation. Yet all of these things, and many others, have been seen and attested to by thousands of people.

With poltergeists the researcher does at least have some physical objects to examine. There are hundreds of testimonies to sort through and dozens of living witnesses to be questioned. That should make it possible to launch a detailed and thorough investigation into the mystery – one that might produce some useful answers. When studying unexplained phenomena such as poltergeists it is important to remember that most people are taken completely by surprise when they are confronted by a seemingly impossible set of circumstances. They display a tendency to remember only a few details of the event, and these are not necessarily the ones that an investigator would find the most useful. The inevitable result is that records tend to be incomplete and partial.

What is needed from a researcher is the ability to identify the features that are common to most or all of the episodes. It is sometimes better to create a 'typical' supernatural event from a vast mass of different accounts than to go into enormous detail in one case. Although bizarre or sensational individual incidents make for good newspaper copy or thrilling horror stories, it is often in the aggregate of cases that the answer may be found. It is with these points in mind that we can now begin to study poltergeist visitations and the poltergeist phenomenon.

# chapter 2

# DEMONS & WITCHES

It would seem that poltergeists have been around since time immemorial. Many ancient books contain descriptions of incidents that the modern researcher would interpret as visitations by poltergeists.

Unfortunately, most of these accounts took the form of small side stories to the main historic events that were being documented. As a result, they miss out many of the details that the modern researcher would find useful. Nevertheless, they serve to show that poltergeists have existed

*'In the name of God, go': some poltergeists are thought by witnesses to be demons or devils, prompting the use of holy water and exorcism rituals in an attempt to get rid of the invisible intruder*

for many centuries and that visitations were much the same a thousand years ago as they are today.

## Demons

Such incidents took place within a different culture to our own, of course. Nobody is free from the prejudices of their time, nor can anyone have knowledge of discoveries and inventions that have not yet been made. It is not surprising, therefore, that some of the earliest incidents were seen as attacks by demons. Take for instance the 'demon' that attacked a farmer living just outside Bingen am Rhein in the year 858 in what is now Germany. The demon began by throwing stones at the farmhouse. A few weeks later it began pounding the walls of the house as if with gigantic invisible hammers, making the walls shake and shudder. After that, the spirit began following the farmer about. Although it was never seen, it might suddenly launch a stream of stones at the farmer wherever he happened to be at the time. The demon then learned how to talk. Somehow it managed to create a voice that boomed out of thin air. It accused the farmer of all manner of sins, including the seduction of a local teenage girl.

The hapless farmer's neighbours soon refused to have him in their houses. The local priest was called in. He decided that the demon was too powerful for him and sent a message to the Bishop of Mainz asking for help and it was this letter that caused the visitation to be recorded in the episcopal annals of Mainz, which have survived the centuries. The bishop sent a team of priests to exorcize the demon. They went to Bingen equipped with sacred relics, Bibles, holy water and detailed instructions from the bishop on how to go about their work. When the priests arrived at the house, they sprinkled holy water all around them and then began their ceremony. All seemed to be going well until the assembled locals began singing a hymn. This provoked a sudden volley of stones, in the middle of which the demon informed everybody that the lead priest from Mainz was an adulterer who lusted after women. The commotion was so great that the priests retreated with their ceremony unfinished. They returned to Mainz to ask for guidance. The annals do not, unfortunately, record what happened next.

## Holy Visitations

Visitations could also be interpreted as the spirits of the dead. In about 1522 (accounts vary) the convent of St Pierre de Lyon suffered a minor scandal when a young nun named Alix de Telieux absconded, taking some jewels with her. A couple of years later news arrived at the convent that the renegade Alix had died. It was said that she had succumbed to the sins of the world – but that detail might simply have been added by the ecclesiastical authorities. Then in 1528 one of the young nuns who had remained at the convent had a strange experience. Anthoinette de Grollée was dozing in her room when she felt somebody lift her veil, kiss her lightly and make the sign of the cross on her forehead. She woke up with a start but after finding nobody in the room she decided that she had imagined it.

A few days later Anthoinette heard the sound of somebody rapping on the floor of her room with their knuckles. There was nobody there and there was not enough space under the floorboards for anyone to be hiding. As the days passed the knocking sound got louder and more frequent. Then it began to follow Anthoinette when she left her room.

Other nuns began to hear it too. The noise was only heard when Anthoinette was present, but she was quite clearly not causing it by any physical means. Eventually young Anthoinette was called in for interrogation by the Mother Superior. The young nun explained about the knocking noises in her room and the feeling of being kissed. She then added that she had been having dreams about the late Alix in recent weeks. The two girls had been close friends before Alix absconded.

The Mother Superior sent a message to the local bishop, who sent a priest named Adrian de Montalembert to the nunnery to investigate. After Montalembert had questioned Anthoinette, it was not long before he heard the mysterious knocking noises for himself. Montalembert decided that the noises were being caused by the unquiet spirit of Alix. He decided to open up communications with the dead nun by calling out questions to her – she could then respond with coded knocks. Once Montalembert began asking questions, the spirit became so communicative as to be almost chatty. It confirmed that it was the spirit of Alix and that it was on some form of temporary release from purgatory so that it could seek salvation. The spirit passed on the lurid details of Alix's sinful life after fleeing the abbey and then it begged for absolution. Finally it asked if Alix's body could be exhumed and reburied in the convent. Only then, said the spirit, would she have demonstrated the forgiveness of those that she had wronged.

After some debate between Montalembert and the Mother Superior, it was agreed that the convent should go to the trouble and expense of exhuming the body and performing the ceremony as requested. The bones were located, dug up and transported to the convent, where they were buried with all the ritual due to a deceased nun of unstained character. For a few days peace reigned and then there began an insistent drumming as if the spirit were demanding communication. Montalembert was called back.

After asking the spirit how it was getting on, he was informed that Alix was now released from purgatory and was free to ascend to heaven. At this point it was noticed that Anthoinette was floating several feet above the ground.

There then came a massive thumping noise that seemed to shake the entire convent to its foundations. This was followed by another such blow, then a third and a fourth. As the hammering blows continued a blazing ball of light erupted in the convent church. It shone out with such incredible brightness that nobody could look at it. After 33 ground-shaking thuds the noise stopped, the light went out and Anthoinette fell to the ground. Silence and peace then reigned at the convent of St Pierre de Lyon. The spirit never returned.

When a visitation took place at the Dominican monastery in Berne, Switzerland it was also seen as a manifestation of a spirit of the dead. However, the outcome was very different in this case. In 1506 a monk named Jetzer went to see his prior with a strange and disturbing story. He said that the bedclothes were being torn off his bed by invisible hands nearly every night. Not only that but he was bothered by noises.

It sounded as if some sort of creature was scrabbling around inside the walls. The prior's initial reaction is not recorded, but within a matter of days he could not ignore the problem. The scrabbling noises had become knocking sounds – no longer confined to Jetzer's cell, they now invaded the entire monastery. No room was free of the noises that came at any time of day or night. Despite the most careful investigation, no explanation could be found.

The prior decided to place holy relics into Jetzer's cell in the hope that they would cure the problem. They made it worse. The noises got louder and then doors began to be flung open and slammed shut with great violence. Stones were lobbed about and objects floated up from tables and drifted across rooms. A disembodied voice then began to mutter unintelligibly, but after a few days it managed to make itself understood. The voice said that it was the spirit of Heinrich Kalpurg who had been the prior in the 1340s. The current prior consulted the monastic records and discovered that there had been a prior of that name at that date. Moreover, he had been expelled for unspecified acts of inefficiency and incompetence. The spirit then announced that he had been a grievous sinner – which was interpreted as being a confession that he had been guilty of embezzling monastic funds, or maybe worse. According to the voice, Kalpurg had fled to Paris where he had been murdered in sordid circumstances.

The prior then ordered continuous masses to be said in the monastery church. God was beseeched to bring peace to the soul of Kalpurg, in order that the monastery might return to normal. The disturbances began to tail off and the monks hoped that their ordeal would soon be over. But events then took a bizarre turn. The prior decided that Jetzer's new-found ability to communicate with the dead would enable him to settle some theological matters. In particular, he wanted to know if the Virgin Mary had been conceived free of original sin. The matter might seem somewhat obscure, but in the early 16th century it was a matter of spirited debate between the Franciscans – who thought that she had – and the Dominicans – who insisted that she had not.

Next time the disembodied voice spoke out in Jetzer's cell the monk asked the prior's question. The voice sounded nonplussed. It said it did not know but it would go and ask St Barbara – a saint that Kalpurg seemed to know quite well in the afterlife. A week later St Barbara appeared in Jetzer's cell, clad in shining white robes. Jetzer asked the question again. St Barbara assured him that she would find out.

After another week had passed St Barbara returned, this time accompanied by two angels. She announced that the Dominicans were right in thinking that the Virgin Mary had not been conceived free of original sin.

Jetzer gave the delighted prior the answer to his question. The fame of the monastery and its visitation spread far and wide. But the local bishop was unconvinced. He sent Jetzer a series of complicated questions that he should ask the saint when she next appeared. His aim was to make sure that she was not an evil spirit in disguise. The saint duly reappeared, along with the two angels. As Jetzer began to ask his questions he started to think that something was wrong. He made a grab for the 'saint', who fought back with remarkably unsaintly vigour. In the rough and tumble that followed, Jetzer unmasked one of the 'angels' as the prior, while the 'saint' and the other angel turned out to be senior monks. The prior assured Jetzer that they had only arranged the stunt to test his credibility – and then he declared that Jetzer had passed the test.

Jetzer seemed to accept the prior's story. Indeed, he appeared to be eagerly awaiting his next saintly visit. This time St Bernard of Clairvaux and St Catherine of Siena had come to see him. After a lengthy interview, 'St Bernard' said he would float out of the window and return to heaven. Jetzer took the saint at his word by grabbing him and bundling him out of the window, only for him to tumble the 15 feet down to the cobbled courtyard. 'St Bernard' was the prior. Jetzer then turned on 'St Catherine', who was trying to scramble out of the door. Realizing that he could not shut the door in time, Jetzer stabbed 'St Catherine' in the leg and so proved 'her' to be the procurator of the monastery in disguise.

The bishop now moved in with the full might of ecclesiastical authority. Jetzer was found guilty of conversing with ghosts and he was expelled from the monastery. He took up the profession of tailoring which he had been learning before becoming a monk. The prior, the procurator and the two other monks who had been unmasked by Jetzer were less fortunate. Convicted of heresy and sacrilege, they were executed. The original cause of all the fuss – the invisible spirit of Prior Kalpurg, with its rappings and its disembodied voice – had been forgotten.

## Witchcraft

Elsewhere it was witches that got the blame for visitations. In February 1658 trouble erupted at a house in Loddington, Northamptonshire. The house was occupied by the elderly and fairly well-to-do Mrs Cowley, her widowed daughter Mrs Stiff and Mrs Stiff's two teenage daughters.

The first sign of trouble was when the two girls began to find that furniture and other objects in their bedroom had been moved while they were out. Naturally they put this down to some servant playing tricks, so they ignored it. Then one night the bedclothes of the two girls were torn off by unseen hands. This woke them up and caused them some fright.

A couple of days later the family were in the parlour when they heard a noise coming from the hall. When they went to see what had caused the commotion they found furniture from the girls' bedroom stacked up by the front door. While they had been out of the parlour a box had been opened and the flax it had contained had been thrown about the room. The servants were called and everything was put straight, but their efforts were in vain. More and more objects began to be moved about the house by the invisible prankster. During a two-week period the flax was removed from the box nearly every day, even when the box was locked shut; a loaf of bread danced around the kitchen of its own accord; one of Mrs Stiff's shoes took to floating about in the upper rooms as if carried by an invisible maid; and an ink pot flew out of the open window of the parlour. When the servant who saw this happen bent down to pick it up he was hit on the head by the stopper. On top of all that, large numbers of stones flew through the windows in both directions. Several hit members of the family and their servants, but nobody was ever hurt. Even when a carving knife was flung at a male servant he came to no harm. The knife reversed itself at the last minute so that the servant was hit by the haft, not the blade.

Other tricks were more destructive. A tub of bran was tipped into a box of salt, so that both were ruined; a large bowl of milk was overturned and all the milk was lost; a barrel of beer was ruined when mud and sand were poured into it; and a tub of peas was overturned and strewn around the storage shed.

So far, however, the trouble had affected only the family and its servants. But things changed on a fateful day in April, when the baker's delivery boy – actually a young man aged about 19 – came to call. He went into the kitchen as usual, put his basket down on the table and stopped for a chat with the cook. However, his cheerful chat came to an abrupt halt when a handful of crumbs from the basket rose slowly into the air, hovered for a moment and then drifted across the room. They scattered themselves all over an unfortunate servant. The baker's boy fled and news of the event spread rapidly. Finally the local magistrate, Mr G Clark, was called in and it was he who took down the details of what had been happening.

The people of 17th-century England were firm believers in witchcraft – with good reason. Most rural areas had a local 'wise woman', or a 'cunning man', who was willing to undertake all sorts of tasks for the locals. These sorcerers made medicines from wild herbs to cure sick cattle, potions to help women in childbirth and ointments to aid healing. Some of these mixtures were highly effective because there are a number of genuinely medicinal wild herbs and plants in the English countryside.

Even if the medicine itself was ineffective, the wise woman could offer remarkably good advice, such as resting for a couple of days. A busy farmer's wife might not usually be able to put her feet up for any

*Lord of the Dance: Old Jenkins made the innkeeper dance quite a jig when he overcharged him for a meal on market day*

length of time, but with the authority of the wise woman behind her few would argue.

Rather more spectacularly, some cunning men or wise women had mastered arts that sound rather like hypnosis. One cunning man, Pigtail Bridger of Crowborough in Sussex, had the ability to paralyse people with a look. Men who incurred his displeasure would find themselves rooted to the spot and unable to move until he told them they could. Another, Old Jenkins of Hereford, took his revenge in another way. When an innkeeper overcharged him for a meal on market day, Old Jenkins ordered the man to dance. The hapless innkeeper involuntarily danced a jig across the floor of his bar for over an hour until Jenkins tired of the sport and broke the spell, allowing the exhausted man to collapse to the floor.

These wise women and cunning men were powerful figures in pre-modern society. They were treated with enormous respect and sometimes with great fear. After all, it was as easy for a cunning man to feed cattle with poison and make them ill as it was for him to cure them of disease. Offering gifts to the local witch or wizard was a wise precaution. Some of these sorcerers traded on this fear by blackmailing local farmers into handing over a portion of their produce.

Witches and wizards are relevant to the study of poltergeists because a number of them were believed to possess what was called a 'familiar'. Some of these creatures looked like imps, demons or fairies and others had the appearance of hares or cats – the origin of the witch's black cat of popular imagination. It was said that they had the power to make themselves invisible. They would then sneak off around the neighbourhood to eavesdrop on what was going on, afterwards reporting back to their master or mistress. It was also thought that familiars did the bidding of the witch or the wizard that controlled them. The deeds ascribed to familiars sound very much like those of poltergeists. They moved furniture about, threw stones, made banging noises and generally disturbed the peace of the person who had incurred the wrath of the familiar's master.

It was as an attack by a familiar that the visitation at Mrs Cowley's house at Loddington was recorded. Once Mr Clark the magistrate was involved, the machinery of the law rolled into action. First of all, the local wise woman was arrested on the charge of sending a familiar to wreak havoc at Mrs Cowley's house. She protested her innocence but she was thrown into prison to await trial. The wise woman said that she had never had a familiar because she had never learned how to control one. She was not believed, of course, and a strict watch was kept on her. However, the upheavals at Mrs Cowley's home continued unabated. On the very day that the witch was imprisoned a cheese exploded into fragments as if a charge of gunpowder had been placed underneath it and set off. The witch was released. As was so often the case with these early accounts, the end of the story is not recorded. We have the report written by Mr Clark up to the release of the witch, but any documents that he wrote subsequently have not survived.

In 1660 another series of paranormal events was blamed on a witch, but once again we do not know how the investigation ended. The case was investigated by Reverend Gibbs, prebendary of Westminster, whose account of the visitation regrettably tails off before the events came to an end. Gibbs was alerted to this instance of 'witchcraft' by an unnamed

*Alarming floor show: during the peak activity of the Bow poltergeist, the upstairs storey of the affected house had to be abandoned by the family due to the violent activity that took place there*

gentleman from Essex. The man said that it had all started when he was doing business with a weaver named Paul Fox, who lived in Bow near Plaistow. A few months before the strange happenings began, he had called on Fox to be given the sad news that the weaver's youngest daughter had died a few days earlier. As she lay on her death bed, the girl had complained that a cold hand had touched her repeatedly on the leg. The Essex gentleman muttered his commiserations, concluded his business and moved on.

Some weeks later the Essex gentleman called again on Fox, but this time he was told that the household was being attacked by witchcraft. The gentleman was sceptical and he said so. At that point an upstairs window opened and a lump of wood was thrown out, missing the man by inches. The man denounced the stunt as 'knavery', whereupon the window opened again and a brick was lobbed out, which the man had to move smartly to avoid. Still convinced that some prankster was throwing the objects, the gentleman pushed past Mr Fox and made straight for the stairs. Fox warned him that the upper part of the house was no place to go. He told the gentleman that he and his family had abandoned the entire top floor a week earlier in order to escape the constant noises and the frequent rain of missiles. The gentleman harrumphed and went on up.

He found himself confronted by a scene of utter mayhem. Numerous items of furniture and clothing were scattered about in confusion and bricks and stones were piled up all over the place. The man stepped over the mess so that he could reach the room overlooking the front door. He thought that the person who had been throwing objects at him must be hiding there. As he pushed the door open, a staff that lay on the floor began to move of its own accord. He stepped forward and stamped his foot down on the object to bring it to a halt. Something must have been making it move, he thought. He picked it up to look for a wire or a thin piece of string. There was no sign of any trickery. That was when a wooden pole lifted itself up from the floor and whacked him over the shoulders.

The man promptly fled from the room, pulling the door shut behind him. As he paused on the landing the door to the room was wrenched open by unseen hands and a mass of clothing, candlesticks and other objects came flying out at him. He ran downstairs to be greeted by the worried Fox family. They all retreated to the kitchen to discuss the terrifying events. Just as they sat down, a clay pipe rose into the air from the sideboard. Then it flew across the room and shattered into a dozen pieces as it hit the wall opposite – the 'witch's familiar' had come downstairs. The Essex gentleman called in Reverend Gibbs, who fortunately knew how to unmask the culprit. He ordained that the object that had moved around the most – a wooden staff – should be slowly roasted over an open fire. This would cause the wizard or the witch who controlled the familiar to come calling, he said. The fire was lit and the staff was placed over it. The Fox family sat down to wait. At first nothing happened and then there was a knock at the door. Paul Fox threw the door open and pounced on the person outside. It turned out to be an elderly woman who lived up the road. She had come to see what the column of smoke was for.

Convinced that they had the witch, Fox and Gibbs tied her up and sent for the magistrate. When the local magistrate arrived he was unimpressed. The old woman was of good character, attended church regularly and was about as far from being a tool of Satan as could be imagined – so he let her go. Gibbs then lost interest in the case so we do not know what happened next.

## The Demon Drummer of Tedworth

Witchcraft was also suspected in what is perhaps the most famous of these early cases: the Demon Drummer of Tedworth. The scene of the visitation was the home of John Mompesson, a wealthy magistrate who lived at Tedworth in Wiltshire. The case caused a sensation and it was thoroughly investigated by clergymen and others. Mr Mompesson himself wrote an account of the visitation after it had ended, which finished with the words:

> *I have been very often of late asked the question whether I have not confessed to his Majesty or any other, a cheat discovered about that affair. To which I gave, and shall to my Dying day give the same answer, That I must bely my self and purjure my self also to acknowledge a cheat in a thing where I am sure there was nor could be any, as I, the Minister of the Peace, and two other Honest Gentlemen deposed at the Assizes, upon my Impleading the praying God to keep me from the same, or the like affliction.*
>
> *And although I am sure this most damnable lye does pass for current amongst one sort of people in the World, invented only, I think, to suppress the Belief of the Being either of God or Devil. Yet I question not but the*

*Thing obtains credit enough amongst those who I principally design should retain a more charitable Opinion of me, than to be any way a deviser of it, only to be talkt of in the World to my own disadvantage and reproach.*

The language is old-fashioned, but Mompesson's indignation is clear. He appears to be adamant that he did not invent the strange happenings or fall for a trick. No doubt he thought that by publishing a true account of the visitation he could quash the more lurid inventions that were circulating. I have based the remainder of this section on Mompesson's comprehensive description of the visitation and the events leading up to it.

In the middle of March 1661 Mompesson was visiting Ludgershall in Wiltshire when the bailiff told him that there was a troublesome beggar in the town. However, two magistrates, Sir William Cawly and Colonel Ayliff, had apparently signed a document that gave the mendicant permission to beg in the streets. The beggar claimed to be a former military drummer in Ayliff's regiment. His habit of beating a drum to attract attention before playing a series of military beats and tattoos to entertain the crowds certainly seemed to support his story. The bailiff, however, found the man a nuisance and wanted him gone.

When Mompesson had the beggar, William Drury, brought before him he asked to see the document that gave him permission to beg. The magistrate quickly concluded that the signatures of Cawly and Ayliff were faked, so he ordered Drury to be thrown into prison and his drum confiscated. He told the bailiff to write to Ayliff asking if Drury really was a retired army drummer of good character, as he claimed. If he was,

Mompesson said, he should be released, together with his drum; if not, he should be charged with vagrancy and illegal begging. Thinking that he had settled the matter, Mompesson got on with his own business in Ludgershall and then went home.

A few days later Drury talked his way out of prison and then disappeared, leaving his drum behind. Not sure what to do with the drum, the bailiff sent it to Mompesson's house, where it was placed in a storeroom and forgotten about. Five weeks later Mompesson went up to London for a few days on business. When he got back he found his family and servants in a state of some excitement. He was told that a gang of thieves had attempted to burgle the house while he had been away. Everyone was convinced that they had heard the sound of men trying to batter the doors down in order to gain access to the house. However, when a male servant had peered out of a window with a gun the noises had ceased. Although the servant had seen no bandits, nobody could think of any other explanation.

Three nights after Mompesson's return the noises resumed. Once again, it sounded as if a number of men were trying to batter the front door in. Mompesson roused his male servants, armed himself with a brace of loaded pistols and opened the door. The noises stopped abruptly. Mompesson walked out into the night, his pistols at the ready, but there was nobody in sight. The front door was then shut and locked, whereupon the same sounds started coming from another door. Once again, Mompesson opened the door and lunged out with loaded pistols. Again the noises stopped and once more there was nobody in sight. Mystified, Mompesson stayed up for a while and then went to bed.

Noises could be heard again on the following night, but this time they were different. The sound of a gang of ruffians trying to break in had given way to the patter of footsteps going across the roof of the house. Mompesson went out into the garden and peered up at the roof. The starlight was bright enough to see by, but he could see nobody moving on top of the house. The sound of nocturnal footsteps on the roof continued for three more nights. Then there was silence for the following three nights. On the fourth night a new sound came. It still seemed to originate from the roof, but it now sounded as if somebody was pounding or thumping with a wooden hammer. The noises lasted for about two hours and then they stopped. This went on for five nights and then it ceased. By this time, Mompesson had noticed that the noises started up just after the family had gone to bed – whether they retired early or late. He suspected that someone, or something, was watching them.

After three peaceful nights the trouble began again. This time the thumping noises began on the roof and then moved to the walls of the house. The sounds moved from side to side and up and down as if whatever was doing the pounding was hovering in front of the walls. After several nights of aimless wandering, the pounding noises began to centre around one particular room – the storeroom where Drury's drum had been put. Then the drum began to play itself. By this time it was August and Mrs Mompesson was getting close to giving birth. As was then usual among the gentry, Mrs Mompesson retired to her bedroom when the due date for the baby approached. At that point the nocturnal noises abruptly ceased. When she had given birth, Mrs Mompesson stayed in her room for three weeks in order to rest, recover and bond with her baby. Then she came downstairs to show the child off to visitors and relatives. That very night the noises began again, but now they were even more terrifying than before.

The noises began as previously, with loud thudding sounds coming from the walls and the roof. But very soon they moved inside the house. It sounded as if some invisible being was thumping its fists against the doors, furniture and walls. Mompesson realized that several of the hammering episodes sounded like military drum beats and calls. This confirmed in him the idea that Drury was somehow to blame. It was very soon obvious that the invisible intruder had lost interest in the drum and had instead developed a fascination with the Mompesson children. None of the accounts state how many children there were, but at least one of them was on the verge of adulthood while the others were younger. Three of the younger children shared a bedroom and it was here that the trouble began to focus. The children's beds would be struck as if with hammers and then the sound of claws scratching the floor would be heard. One night the children's beds were lifted more than two feet up into the air. They were then allowed to fall back to the floor with a terrific crash. Mompesson tried moving the children to a new room but it did no good – the invisible intruder merely followed them.

On 5 November the visitation entered a new phase. It began in the children's room in the middle of the morning. A servant was tidying up the mess from the night before when he saw a wooden board twitch and move. 'Give it to me,' said the man. The board promptly floated up into the air as if carried by unseen hands and then it drifted slowly towards the servant. It stopped when it was about a yard from him. The servant called

*Left in the storeroom, Drury's drum seemed to be the likely source of unnerving noises*

out for Mompesson, who came into the room. 'Nay,' said the servant. 'Let me have it in my hand.' The wooden board then drifted closer and came to rest in his outstretched palm. He put the board down, but it instantly sprang into the air again and placed itself between his fingers. This happened no fewer than 20 times, at which point Mompesson told the servant to leave the room. As the servant left there was a sudden and overpowering stench of burning sulphur.

Sulphur being considered to be the smell of hell, Mompesson sent for the local vicar, Mr Cragg. The vicar suggested that a prayer meeting might solve the problem. He then rounded up a group of intrepid neighbours, who were willing to take on in prayer what was by now being called the 'Demon Drummer'. When Mr Cragg arrived the drumming and pounding noises first sounded out from several rooms, but then retreated to the children's bedroom. Mr Cragg led Mompesson and the group of neighbours up to the bedroom. As soon as Cragg knelt down and began to pray, the noises stopped. Encouraged, the neighbours joined in the prayers. When the praying finished, Cragg stood up and turned to say something to Mompesson.

As he did so a chair in the corner of the room began walking forwards on its own. Then a wooden chest started bouncing up and down. The children's shoes leapt out of the cupboard where they were stored, rose about six feet above the floor and then began flying back and forth across the room. The chair continued its advance towards the minister, but it seems to have been only a distraction – a wooden board came up and hit him from behind while he was staring at the walking chair. To his great surprise, the wooden board did not hurt him at all. All he felt was a gentle nudge. As the mayhem continued Cragg and the others fled, leaving Mompesson to face the invisible intruder alone.

Having decided that some sort of decisive action was needed, Mompesson split the children up and sent each of them to stay with a different relative. He hoped that the Demon Drummer would not be able to torment them all at the same time. The plan worked because most of the children were left alone – only Mompesson's ten-year-old daughter was troubled. Early in December, the magistrate brought the children home and changed the family's sleeping arrangements. Mrs Mompesson and the baby slept in one room, the children who did not seem to be affected slept in a second and Mompesson shared a room with the ten-year-old girl. These changes seem to have produced an alteration in the behaviour of the intruder. The loud banging and thumping noises decreased in volume and tempo, but now objects began to move about when nobody was watching. A Bible was frequently moved to the fireside from its place on a shelf, while clothes belonging to Mr Mompesson's mother were taken out of their wardrobe and dumped on the floor.

One day a friend of old Mrs Mompesson's came to visit. The woman said that she had heard of a fairy that had been in the habit of visiting a house in a village a few miles away. It had moved things about in a similar way, but it had also left money behind as if to make up for the nuisance it had caused. Old Mrs Mompesson said that she would be pleased if their drummer would leave money behind. And for the next few days the drumming was replaced by the sound of coins being counted out or jingled in a pouch. To Mrs Mompesson's disappointment, though, no money was ever found.

A household servant named John then went to Mr Mompesson and told him that he had noticed an odd thing. Whenever he was holding a knife or a sword, the intruder would cease its activities. Next time the drumming began Mompesson tested the theory. He got John to pick up a sword, whereupon the noises ceased abruptly. This rather curious ploy worked for the rest of the visitation. If the household wanted peace, all that was needed was for John to enter the troubled room carrying a sword.

However, he fell asleep one night while he was holding a sword in his hand. As soon as it slipped from his fingers the pounding noises immediately began. When he bent down to pick the sword up it sprang away from him as if it had been kicked away. This happened twice before he managed to grab it, after which the noises again ceased.

In January 1662 something new happened. The sound of a man singing began to be heard. The eerie voice could usually be heard high up in a chimney. At about the same time a glowing ball of blue light began to be seen at night, gliding gently and silently from room to room. It seemed to be looking for something – or someone. On 10 January Sir Thomas Chamberlain of Oxford arrived with a group of gentlemen. He had come to investigate matters. The new arrivals experienced all of the usual tricks of the Demon Drummer and then a new stunt began – the sound of rustling silk and dainty footsteps was heard, as if a lady in a silk dress were walking through the house in high heels.

One night, one of Sir Thomas's companions decided to challenge the intruder. As the sounds of drumming moved through the house the man called out in a firm voice.

*All hell let loose? A peak in the Tedworth visitation came when a chair and a chest of drawers came to life and shoes flew across the children's bedroom at exactly the same time*

'Drummer,' he cried, 'if Satan hath set thee to work give three knocks and no more.'

There then came three incredibly loud knocks, after which there was no more activity for several hours.

A few days later the family Bible was found lying on the floor. It was open at Mark, Chapter 3, which referred to Jesus being able to cast out demons.

By the middle of 1662 the intensity and frequency of the disturbances was fading, but they continued to erupt from time to time. Sometimes a voice would shout out, 'A witch, a witch.' At other times the drumming would return for a few nights or phantom footsteps would be heard around the house. One night John the servant found himself confronted by what looked like a black shadow in the size and shape of a man with two glowing red eyes.

Then in April 1663 came startling news from Gloucester. William Drury had been arrested for theft, but before he had been brought to trial a most amazing thing had happened. When Drury discovered that a man from Wiltshire was visiting the prison he called the visitor over to his cell.

'What news is there from Wiltshire?' asked Drury.

'Why none of concern to thee,' replied the visitor.

Drury chuckled. 'Oh, no,' he scoffed. 'Do not you hear of the drumming at a gentleman's house in Tedworth?'

'That I do, well enough,' replied the visitor quickly.

'Aye,' said Drury boastfully. 'I have plagued him and he shall never be at quiet till he hath made me satisfaction for taking away my drum.'

The man from Wiltshire hurried to tell the magistrates about the exchange. As a result Drury was sent off to the courts in Salisbury to stand trial for witchcraft. Mompesson himself appeared as a witness to testify to the mayhem that had been disturbing his house. In his account Mompesson recorded:

> *I indicted him as a felon for the supposed witchcraft about my house. The Assizes came on, where I indicted him on the Statute Primo Jacobi cap.12. Where you may find that to feed, imploy, or reward any evil spirit is Felony. And the Indictment against him was that he did* quendam malum spiritum negotiare. *The grand Jury found the Bill upon the evidence, but the petty Jury acquitted him.*

Despite this, Drury was convicted of being a vagabond and sentenced to be transported to the West Indies to work as a slave on the sugar plantations. As at Ludgershall, however, he somehow got out of prison and again vanished from view.

By this time the Demon Drummer of Tedworth had become so famous that Charles II himself had taken an interest. He sent Lord Falmouth and Lord Chesterfield down to investigate. Nothing untoward happened during the few days that the gentlemen were present, but then all of the accounts agree that things were calming down in any case. It was probably this abortive visit that led to the rumours that the disturbances had never actually taken place. Some even said that they had been the result of some sort of trickery on the part of Mompesson or a member of his household. After the two courtiers had left there were a few further events, but they were minor compared to what had gone before. By the autumn of 1663, whatever had been causing the problems had gone. The Demon Drummer of Tedworth was no more.

## The Ringcroft Events

Other poltergeist attacks did, however, continue but witchcraft was not always seen as the culprit. The strange events that took place over a four-month period in 1695 at Ringcroft in Galloway, Scotland came in for as much attention as did the Demon Drummer of Tedworth. This time, however, those on the receiving end of the visitation chose to blame a 'spirit' for the trouble. The case was thoroughly investigated by the local minister, Andrew Ewart, who at various times called in four other ministers to help him, assisted by two local lairds and several gentlemen.

The centre of the visitation was the humble home of Andrew Mackie, a stonemason who lived in the village of Ringcroft. As was so often the case, the victims had not realized that something odd was happening until several unexplained events had taken place. Mackie later stated that the trouble had begun one night in February 1695. All of his cattle had escaped from their shed because the ropes holding them in their stalls had been cut or torn. At the time he had blamed intruders. A few days later something else had happened. On that occasion he had found one cow tied so tightly to a roof beam that its hooves were barely touching the ground and it was almost choking.

It was on the night of 7 March that the family realized that something supernatural was afoot. A number of stones were thrown around the house by invisible hands. The doors and the windows were locked and every room was searched, but still the unseen assailant threw stones about. The Mackie family soon discovered that no matter how large the stones were, or how fast they flew through the air, they did no damage when they hit a person or an object. Anyone who was struck by one of the stones felt that somebody had gently pushed it against them and then let it fall.

On 10 March the four children were about to enter the house when nobody else was at home, but they stopped dead in their tracks when they saw what looked like a human figure. It was sitting hunched up in front of the fireplace, wrapped up in a blanket. The youngest boy, aged ten, recognized the blanket as being his own. 'We have nothing to fear if we bless ourselves first,' he told his siblings. When they still hung back, the boy said a brief prayer and then stepped boldly forward. He grabbed the blanket and gave it a tug. The cloth came away easily, leaving nothing behind but empty air and a stool.

On the following day the minister came to say prayers in the house. He was assailed by a shower of stones. The barrage soon stopped and his prayers were completed. There was no further trouble for a week, but on 18 March the stone throwing began again. The minister was unable to return to the house himself, so he asked Charles Maclellan, laird of Colline, to go in his place. Colline recorded the following statement:

*I went to the house, where the spirit molested me mightily, threw stones and divers other things at me, and beat me several times on the shoulders and sides with a great staff so that those who were present heard the noise of the blows. That same night it pulled me off the side of a Bed, knocked upon the Chests and Boards as People do at a Door. And as I was at Prayer leaning*

> *on the side of a bed, I felt something thrusting my arm up and casting my eyes thitherward perceived a little white Hand and Arm from the Elbow down, but it vanished presently.*

In early April the visitation took a turn for the worse. Bundles of burning straw began to appear around the farm, apparently out of nowhere. At first the fires were confined to the stone-flagged yard, and so did no harm, but then lumps of burning peat began to be thrown instead of stones. One lodged in the thatched roof of a sheep house, which then burned down. Then a lump of stone fell on to a bed shared by two of the children. It was so hot that it scorched a hole in the bedclothes before it could be kicked off. Two hours later it was still too hot to hold.

On 8 April Mackie was digging in his garden when he found some bones. He alerted the local magistrate, who at once concluded that the bones must belong to a murder victim. His theory was that the ghost of the deceased person must be causing all of the trouble. Colline was again called in, but despite the most rigorous inquiries no hint of a missing person with any connection to the house could be found.

Then on 9 April Ewart, the local minister, summoned four fellow ministers to the house for an exorcism. The ritual had only just started when the ministers were hit by a deluge of stones. Ewart ignored the attack and continued. But then something lifted him up into the air and pushed him forward, so that he fell flat on his face. Undeterred, he managed to finish his service. Unfortunately, it had no noticeable effect.

For several days objects were moved around, stones were thrown and burning peat was hurled in all directions. Then on 26 April the 'spirit' began to talk. 'Ye all be witches,' it announced. 'And I shall take thee down to Hell.' After uttering several other threats the voice turned suddenly more gentle. 'Thou shalt be troubled till Tuesday,' it declared.

On the following Tuesday Colline was again present, having been told about the prediction that the spirit voice had made. When noises began coming from the barn, Colline led Mackie to the doorway and both men peered in. According to Colline:

> *We observed a black thing in the corner of the same. It increased gradually as if it would have filled the whole House; we could not discern any distinct Form it had, but only that it resembled a black Cloud. It was very frightening to them all and threw barley and mud in their faces.*

And then suddenly the thing was gone, never to return.

## The Cock Lane Ghost

The cases that we have so far examined remain mysterious and unexplained, even though they were seen as the work of ghosts, witches or demons in their time. However, a mysterious haunting that caught the public imagination in 1762 appears to have been satisfactorily explained in the same year. The train of events that led to the Cock Lane Ghost, as the visitation came to be known, began in 1756 when William Kent married Elizabeth Lynes in Norfolk. The couple then moved to London, but a year later Elizabeth died in childbirth. Her sister Fanny moved to London to care for the baby and to act as housekeeper for Kent. The baby died of some unspecified illness a few months later – not an uncommon occurrence at the time – but by this time Fanny and Kent had fallen in love.

The law did not permit them to marry at that time but nothing could stop them setting up house together. They occupied the upper floors of a property in Cock Lane which were rented from the man who lived on the ground floor, a Mr Richard Parsons. Being short of cash, Parsons borrowed £20 from Kent. He agreed to pay the sum back at a rate of a pound each month. By the autumn of 1761 Fanny was pregnant, so when Kent had to go away from London for a couple of weeks on business she did not want to be left alone. Her solution was to invite her landlord's 11-year-old daughter Elizabeth to stay with her while Kent was away.

One night, a strange noise was heard in the Kent apartment. At first it sounded as if a large rat was scurrying about behind the wooden panelling, but then it began to sound more like human knuckles banging on wood. It was rather odd. On the next night the sounds came back, but this time they were louder and more insistent. By the time Kent returned from London Fanny was in a state of great fear. She had somehow become convinced that the noises were caused by a demon that had come to kill her.

Kent could see no alternative but to move, so he took rooms in Bartlett Court, Clerkenwell. Before leaving, he asked Parsons for the return of his money. Parsons refused to pay him back and then he taunted Kent with the fact that he was living with Fanny out of wedlock. He threatened to write to Fanny's family in Norfolk and reveal what was going on. Kent consulted his lawyers and launched a legal action to get his money back.

Meanwhile, the move to Clerkenwell proved to be disastrous. Within days Fanny had contracted smallpox and a few days later she was dead. Back in Cock Lane, the strange noises continued. The sounds migrated downstairs from the former Kent room to Elizabeth's bedroom. They were most noticeable at night, when she was in bed, but they would start at all sorts of hours. However, it was soon noticed that they could only be heard when Elizabeth was in the house.

Parsons began charging people to enter his house so that they could listen to the inexplicable noises. Among those who came were Dr Johnson, the Duke of York, Horace Walpole and the Reverend Douglas, who was later to become Bishop of Salisbury. A woman named Mary Frazer was hired to be a sort of chaperone to young Elizabeth. Parsons was perhaps concerned by the fact that a number of strange men went in and out of her bedroom at night. After a few weeks the attraction of the odd noises began to wane and the visitors tailed off. Perhaps in an effort to save her job, Frazer then hit upon the idea of allowing people to question the 'ghost'. She suggested that the ghost should give one knock to mean 'yes' and two knocks to mean 'no'. If it chose not to answer or did not know the answer, it should make a scratching noise.

The new system proved to be an enormous hit and soon crowds of paying visitors were flocking to Cock Lane. Over the course of the autumn of 1761 the ghost gradually shared a harrowing story with the stream of visitors. It revealed that it was the spirit of the recently departed Fanny – even though the noises had begun when Fanny was very much alive. Quickly dubbed 'Scratching Fanny' by the London crowd, the entity then began to discuss the details of Fanny's relationship with Kent. Most of these were salacious, but one claim stood out boldly. Scratching Fanny declared that she had been murdered by Kent, who had daily dosed her drink with arsenic. She had not succumbed to smallpox after all. When the visitors asked what should be done about the claims, the ghost replied that Kent should hang.

Inevitably news of the accusations reached Kent. He demanded that Parsons and Elizabeth retract the claims. They countered that the claims came from Fanny's ghost, not from themselves. Kent was invited to Cock Lane, so that he could question the spirit himself. After some debate about who should be in attendance at the event and how it should be conducted, Kent went to Elizabeth's bedroom in Cock Lane. At first the ghost refused to make any noises. It had been growing noticeably quieter in recent weeks, but after a while the familiar knockings began.

Kent examined the bedroom for signs of trickery and then the Reverend John Moore began to question the spirit. After some preliminary queries, Moore got to the main business.

'Are you Fanny Lynes?' he asked. There came one knock for 'yes'.

'Were you murdered by William Kent?' There was another single knock for 'yes'.

'Did anyone else assist Kent?' Two knocks indicated 'no'.

William Kent leapt to his feet. 'Thou art a lying spirit,' he shouted and then he stormed out. He then went to see his lawyers, where he launched a prosecution against Parsons, Elizabeth, Frazer and Moore, on the grounds of conspiracy to slander.

The case progressed and by June 1762 it came to court. The matter revolved around whether a disembodied spirit was making the accusations or whether Parsons was producing the noises. If the 'ghost' episode was shown to be a hoax it would prove that the accusations against Kent were false. Perhaps it was all an attempt to dissuade Kent from pursuing his case for the repayment of the £20.

The court made three journeys to Elizabeth's bedroom. On each occasion the court officials undertook a strict search to make sure that no trickery was possible. On the first two visits no noises were heard. The magistrate leading the investigation told Parsons that unless something happened on the third visit he would be found guilty.

When the court made their final trip the spirit repeated its story about the murder. But this time there was something different about the sounds. Elizabeth's bed was searched and a piece of wood was found. The girl had been rapping with the wood.

Next day the court found for Kent. Parsons, Frazer and Moore were condemned to stand in the pillory. The news of Elizabeth's attempted trickery spread rapidly and made all the newspapers of the day. So far as 18th-century London was concerned, the concept of ghosts had been thoroughly debunked. Other visitations still took place, but none of them were investigated properly nor were the events recorded carefully. Educated men no longer took them seriously. As a result, some of the accounts that survive are sketchy and superficial while others are solely concerned with disproving the notion of ghosts.

## The Bell Witch

However, people in the United States remained rather more open to the idea of the supernatural. As a result, the visitation that affected the

Bell family of Robertson County, Tennessee has been recorded in much greater detail than would have been the case in England. The Bell family consisted of John Bell, his wife Lucy and their nine children. They lived in an isolated wooden farmhouse some distance from anything that might be termed a town. Four of the children – John, the eldest, 12-year-old Elizabeth (known as Betsy), ten-year-old Richard and nine-year-old Joel – were affected more than the others.

The visitation seems to have begun in the early months of 1817, though the initial manifestations were so minor and sporadic that it is impossible to be certain. One night the family was disturbed by what sounded like rats or other small animals scuffling about the house. On another occasion, the noises sounded more like a dog scrabbling at the front door. These animal sounds gradually escalated in intensity. By the autumn of 1817 the whole family was aware that something odd was going on. But nothing could be seen. They found that if they got up in the night to investigate the sounds, they could find nothing. If a lamp was lit the noises ceased immediately. No matter what steps were taken, no rats were ever found. It was a real puzzle but at that stage it was still not much of a problem.

That changed in the spring of 1818, when loud thumps and bangs echoed through the farmhouse. Soon afterwards a rather disturbing sound began to be heard. It was difficult to place at first, but the Bells soon decided that it sounded very much like a person smacking his lips in anticipation of a feast. Next came a sound that was more akin to somebody being throttled. It was most upsetting, but worse was to come.

The first physical manifestation took place one night – the bedclothes were hauled off the beds in which the children slept. This happened on several consecutive nights. It woke the children and caused an understandable degree of fright and alarm. After a couple of weeks of restless nights, events escalated when Richard was woken up by something pulling hard on his hair. His screams roused the household, which ensured another broken night's sleep. Then it was Joel's turn. Finally the poltergeist turned on Betsy – her hair was pulled night after night.

It soon became clear that having found Betsy, the invisible intruder had found its target. Not only was her hair pulled repeatedly, but stones were thrown at her – even when she was indoors and nobody else was in the room. Then an invisible hand slapped her face. Her brother, who was talking to her at the time, heard the slap and saw Betsy's cheek redden where the blow had fallen.

This was too much for John Bell. He sent for a near neighbour named James Johnson, who knew his Bible rather better than most people did. It seems that Johnson began by thinking that the children were playing some rather cruel tricks on their father. However, he could not make up his mind if Betsy was in on the prank or was a victim.

When Johnson called at the Bell household all was quiet for a while, but then there came the familiar sound of smacking lips. Johnson swung round angrily. 'Stop it. In the name of the Lord,' he shouted. The sound stopped and nothing else happened during his visit.

The persecution of Betsy continued after Johnson had left. Johnson advised John Bell to arrange for a rota of neighbours to be in the house, where they could keep an eye on things – on the children, in other words. The stone throwing, the face slapping and the knocks and bangs continued unabated, but at least there were witnesses from outside the family. When one visitor expressed the view that the events were all some kind of children's trick he was promptly slapped on the face by an invisible hand.

The disturbances then moved outside the house. They began on the track that led to the local church and the school. About a hundred yards from the house the track passed a dense thicket of trees and bushes. As the children walked past this thicket on their way to and from school they would find themselves struck by a flying stick. In common with the stones that had been thrown at Betsy, however, they either missed the children or only touched them lightly if they hit their target. Young Joel took to throwing the sticks back, but they were returned with increased force. It seemed that something in the bushes was catching them. Using his pocket knife (children had such things then), Richard marked a stick and threw it at the thicket – the marked stick came swishing back in an instant. There had to be somebody there. However, when the thicket was searched there was no sign of life.

Back indoors the team of neighbours had become so accustomed to the invisible intruder that they started to play games with it. When they began by tapping on the kitchen table the intruder immediately responded with an identical number of raps. Young Richard later wrote that this behaviour had only made things worse. It had made the spirit seek attention, rather in the manner of a naughty child. Soon, the familiar lip-smacking and choking noises began to be accompanied by grunts, groans, whistles and whispers. At first the whispers could not be understood – they were too

*Children living near the Bell farm found that if they threw a stick into a bush, the Bell Witch would usually throw it back at them. It soon became their favourite game*

faint and indistinct – but within a few days it was possible to discern words and phrases. One of the ghost's first utterings was 'I am a spirit who was once happy. But I have been disturbed and am now unhappy.' The majority of the voice's comments were altogether less pleasant and less informative. Many of them were unprintable, expressing views that few would air in public. John Bell refused to write down most of what the voice said on the grounds that it was blasphemous or of an explicitly sexual nature. The voice expressed its hatred of John Bell, whom it called 'Old Jack Bell', saying that it had come to torment him.

The threat was not idle, for the entity soon turned away from Betsy and focused its attention on John. In addition to the slapping and the stone-throwing, John mysteriously contracted a locked jaw and a swollen tongue. He could sometimes neither eat nor talk for days on end. John Bell was not the only member of the household to come in for harsh treatment. The family had a young slave called Anky, who helped Mrs Bell out with household tasks such as the washing and the cleaning.

The voice would sometimes follow Anky about the house, making comments that today would be classed as racist. The spirit also resorted to more conventional insults. On one occasion the unfortunate girl found herself deluged with a liquid that looked like spit.

When it was asked for more details of who or what it was, the voice at first replied that it was a Native American who had been buried on the site of the house. The visitation was a protest against the building of a white folks' farm on top of its bones, it said. It then discarded that explanation and declared that it was 'Old Kate Batts's Witch'. Kate Batts was a local black woman who earned a modest living as a sort of doctor-cum-social worker to the black community. She acted as a midwife at births, laid out the dead ready for funerals, prepared herbal remedies for the sick and lent a sympathetic ear to those with troubles. Kate Batts was called in for questioning, but she steadfastly denied having anything to do with the upheavals at the Bell household. Fortunately for her, she was believed. She also denied using witchcraft of any type at all, but the voice's insistence that it was 'Old Kate Batts's Witch' stuck in people's minds. Thereafter, the phenomenon came to be called the Bell Witch.

Within a few weeks the voice of the Bell Witch had been joined by others. A gruff male voice declared that its name was Blackdog, a young boy's voice said it was Jerusalem and a woman's voice claimed to be Mathematics. The four voices took to singing bawdy tavern songs and telling rude jokes, while the smell of whisky filled the house. It was as if some loud drunken party was being enjoyed by the Bell Witch and its friends. The voices began to discuss local people with a frankness that was deeply embarrassing. Medical problems were talked about, as well as the sexual behaviour of married couples. Then the voices began to make accusations of drunkenness, violence and theft, none of which could be either proved or disproved.

Needless to say, they caused understandable upset and merriment in the community. The voices then took to repeating long passages from the local minister's Sunday sermon, mocking and joking all the way.

One day, the voice of the Bell Witch announced that it knew the location of a secret hoard of hidden gold. It then whispered the details to Betsy. The boys of the family took shovels and spent hours digging at the specified spot, but they found nothing. When they got back the

Bell Witch broke out into loud laughter and teased the boys about the escapade for days. It had obviously enjoyed the joke.

The Bell Witch enjoyed other unpleasant jokes, too, such as placing pins in beds or on chairs, where people might be expected to prick themselves. The witch also developed a kind of fascination with shoes. They were moved about when nobody was looking and they were wrenched off people's feet when they sat down.

John Bell was the target of the majority of the incidents and he also came in for the most unpleasant treatment. One attack was worse than the rest. He had just stepped out of the front door to begin work on the farm for the day when the Bell Witch grabbed his feet and would not let him walk. Suddenly he felt the invisible hands let go, but he was then punched so hard in the face that he staggered back and had to sit down on a log to recover. The Bell Witch then threw John off the log and shrieked with laughter as it jerked his arms and legs about. He had no means of controlling his convulsive movements. When the invisible entity finally let him go, it stayed in the vicinity singing obscene and offensive songs. Richard had just joined his father so he helped him back indoors, where he took to his bed for a couple of days.

Aggressive as the Bell Witch was towards the father of the family, it could be surprisingly pleasant to the rest of the household. When Mrs Bell was taken ill, the voice hung about weeping and lamenting, 'Poor Lucy. Oh, poor Lucy.' Then it made a couple of pounds of hazelnuts appear at the side of the sick bed. When Betsy saw the nuts she commented, 'Oh, but we have no nutcrackers.' Instantly two pounds of shelled hazel nuts arrived. The sick woman did not fancy the nuts – they are not generally known as a suitable invalid food – so the Bell Witch came back with a large bunch of grapes, which fell from nowhere on to Mrs Bell's bed. The voice said, 'These will be good for her health,' as the grapes landed.

On Betsy's birthday the Bell Witch proved to be very generous. A large basket of fruit, including oranges, bananas and grapes, materialized out of nowhere. 'Those came from the West Indies,' the witch announced. 'I brought them myself.' It sounded almost proud.

In 1819 Betsy fell in love with a local farm boy named Joshua Gardner. By this time, the disturbances had been going on for about two years. The romance blossomed and an engagement was thought to be imminent. Suddenly the Bell Witch seemed to become aware of the relationship. Not only that, it took a violent dislike to it. The voice of the Bell Witch began following Betsy around the house. It said things like, 'Please, Betsy Bell, don't have Joshua Gardner,' or 'Don't marry Joshua Gardner' – and then it tried insulting the hapless young man.

When such pleading did not work, the voice tried a new tactic. When Betsy was out with Gardner, the Bell Witch would keep up a running commentary for the benefit of the rest of the Bell family. It repeated the conversation the two were having, it announced when they were kissing and it described where Joshua put his hands and how Betsy reacted. When Betsy came home, the voice taunted her for her supposedly wanton ways. In the end the pressure got too much and the couple broke up.

Next day one of Joshua's friends arrived at the Bell farm in a blazing temper. Frank Miles pushed his way into the house and shouted out, 'Take any shape you desire, just so that I can get my hands on you.' There followed a few seconds of silence, before an invisible fist punched the young man extremely hard in the face and then in the stomach, causing him to double up in pain and gasp for breath. He left when he had recovered from the beating. The activities of the Bell Witch were heading toward the climax that would ensure its contemporary fame and make it one of the most startling cases in the history of poltergeist studies. On 18 December 1820 John Bell announced that he was not feeling well and that he was going to bed early. Next day he did not wake up and he was found to be in a stupor. The voice of the Bell Witch gloated: 'It's useless for you to try to relieve Old Jack. I've got him this time. He will never get up from that bed again.'

After John junior had sent for the doctor he noticed a small bottle that neither he nor anyone else recognized. The Bell Witch spoke out again.

'I put it there. And I gave Old Jack a dose last night while he was asleep, which fixed him.'

The father of the tormented family died the next day without regaining consciousness. On the day of the funeral the witch moved around the house singing songs, one of which was the then popular bar room ditty 'Row me up some brandy, Oh'.

The apparent murder of John Bell spread the fame of the Bell Witch far and wide. This single act has ensured that the case remains so famous today. No other poltergeist has ever been known to cause the death of a person – or even inflict serious injury. But then the Bell Witch had punched and hit several different people before John Bell died, so it seems to have been abnormal. After the funeral, the Bell Witch went relatively quiet. All of its usual antics were performed, but everybody agreed that they were neither as spectacular nor as frequent as they had been before.

On one occasion, John junior asked the Bell Witch if it could help him to speak to the spirit of his dead father. The Bell Witch refused. 'He is no longer of this world,' it said. After explaining that any evidence of a person surviving death was fraudulent it then instructed John junior to look out of the window. He did so and saw a set of footprints being made in the snow, as if an invisible man were approaching the house. The Bell Witch claimed that the prints were identical to those made by Old Jack Bell in his winter boots. Young John did not bother checking. He had lost interest.

A few weeks later the Bell family was at supper when a loud crashing and rumbling noise came from the chimney. What looked like a large cannonball thumped into the fireplace. It then rolled into the room and exploded in a cloud of choking smoke. The voice of the Bell Witch boomed out, 'I am going and will be gone for seven years.' The smoke cleared and the Bell Witch had gone.

Seven years later it was back. By this time only Mrs Lucy Bell and her two youngest children were living in the farmhouse – the other children had married and moved away. The manifestations began as before, with the sounds of invisible animals scratching about. On a couple of nights bedclothes were torn off again. Mrs Bell and her children decided to ignore anything that happened. They did not even discuss the Bell Witch in the house. After a few days the manifestations ceased. John junior claimed that when the disturbances ceased for the second time he heard the voice of the Bell Witch say that it was leaving for 107 years. By that reckoning it should have been back in 1935, but there is no record of it reappearing.

# Analysing the Early Evidence

Looking back on these early cases it is clear that they contain many of the features that are now associated with poltergeist visitations. The first fact that any researcher must face is that at least two of these cases involved obvious and proven trickery by the humans involved. At Berne some of the monks pretended to be ghosts and spirits in order to provide Jetzer with messages that they wanted to be taken as the pronouncements of the saints. In the Cock Lane visitation, young Elizabeth Parsons was caught rapping her knuckles on a piece of wood in order to produce knocking noises. At this distance in time it is impossible to know whether the earlier manifestations in these two cases were also fraudulent or whether the visitations had begun as genuinely paranormal events that were then manipulated by the humans.

Nor do we know if the other cases were genuine or not, even though no fakery was detected. We have to read the records as they stand and judge them accordingly.

Fraud apart, all of the visitations shared one characteristic – they took place in people's homes. Poltergeists do not infest streets or open fields. The presence of humans on a daily and prolonged basis seems to be necessary. They also seem to require the presence of one particular human being if they are to appear. In the Cock Lane visitation it was young Elizabeth Parsons, in the convent of St Pierre de Lyon it was Anthoinette de Grollée, while at the Dominican monastery in Berne it was the monk Jetzer. Modern researchers term this central person the 'focus'. The throwing of stones was also common to each visitation. So prevalent is the throwing of stones that some researchers maintain that a visitation is not really that of a poltergeist unless some stones are thrown about. Although these early accounts do not comment on the types of stone that are thrown, evidence from more recent cases suggests that the poltergeist uses stones that have been picked up at the site of their visitation.

A further feature is shared in almost all of the cases. Although the stones and the other objects that are thrown about are often moved with great speed and violence, when they strike a person they do so gently and they rarely leave a bruise. However, when they hit a wall or a floor – as did the clay pipe in the home of the weaver Paul Fox – they will break or shatter. It is almost as if the poltergeist is determined to get attention, but does not actually want to hurt anybody. The Bell Witch was unusual in actually inflicting injury. Knocks, bangs and raps also occur in most of these early cases. They may vary in volume and number, but nearly every poltergeist will make such noises at some point during the visitation.

It can also be noticed that nearly all of the visitations began quietly and then built up in intensity as time passed. Because of that, the people who were experiencing a visitation did not realize what was happening until things had reached a reasonably advanced stage. The pattern of disturbances only became clear with hindsight. In the Bell Witch case these early events had been mistaken for rats moving about. This conclusion had also been reached at the start of the Cock Lane visitation. The Tedworth visitation was unusual in that the very first events were loud, frightening and unmistakably odd.

In some cases, the events appeared to build up to a spectacular climax and then cease abruptly; in others, there was a gradual escalation of events, followed by an equally slow decline. Perhaps these impressions are down to faulty recording – in several instances the documents that we have do not tell the whole story. As with modern events, most of the visitations in these early accounts involve no apparition of any kind. Things move and noises are heard, but nothing is seen. When an apparition does appear, it tends to be shadowy and fleeting. A vague black cloud was seen in the Ringcroft case and an indistinct black figure appeared in the Tedworth visitation. Both of them lasted for only a few seconds.

Some of the people in these early visitations attempted to communicate with the poltergeist. In some cases this was achieved by persuading the poltergeist to reply to a series of questions by using a knock code. Other poltergeists developed a voice so that they could speak directly to humans. The disembodied voice seems to be rather more common in the early cases, but that might be because only the more spectacular visitations got written down. One interesting feature of the communications is that they tend toward the sensational and the obscene. When the poltergeist talks about itself, it is usually in terms of murder, crime and exotic sexual escapades. Jetzer's poltergeist claimed to be a former prior of the monastery who had been dismissed in disgrace and then murdered; the Cock Lane Ghost also claimed to have been murdered; and the spirit claiming to be that of the disgraced nun Alix de Telieux poured out an enormously colourful account of her sinful life after leaving the convent. No poltergeist has ever claimed to have been a respectable person who has led an utterly blameless and routine life.

However, where the story of the poltergeist could be tested, it proved to be false. The Cock Lane Ghost claimed to be the ghost of a person who had been alive when the disturbances began, while the Bell Witch made various claims about itself which were evidently paradoxical.

Another feature of the claims made by early poltergeists about themselves is that they all fitted in very closely with the views of the people on the receiving end of a visitation. For instance, the nuns of St Pierre de Lyon believed that the human soul survived bodily death and that those who had committed sins would go to purgatory before being admitted to heaven – so the poltergeist claimed to be exactly such a soul. The Tedworth visitation occurred at a time when belief in witches as assistants of the devil was at a high point, so the poltergeist ran through the house screaming, 'A witch. A witch.' And when Mr Mompesson thought that the drumming beggar William Drury might be to blame, the poltergeist began playing Drury's confiscated drum.

At the time of the Tedworth visitation, it caused a sensation when Drury confessed that he had used witchcraft to cause the mayhem at Mompesson's house. In the event, however, Drury was acquitted of witchcraft at his trial. The records of the trial have not survived, so we do not know what evidence was brought nor why he was acquitted, which is a great shame. It seems obvious, though, that even at that time the evidence was not considered strong enough. There has been some debate among modern researchers as to whether Drury caused the events at Mompesson's house. If so, did he use paranormal means or more mundane tactics? Perhaps it was just that Drury had heard of the Demon Drummer and thought he would try a bit of blackmail. After all, he had a grudge against Mompesson. When all was said and done, Drury was just a beggar who sought alms by claiming to be a retired army drummer. He was not considered to be a wizard, nor did he pretend to be one.

The Bell Witch ceased its visitation in 1828. Just 16 years later a new visitation would capture headlines around the world. It would seem to solve the poltergeist enigma.

# chapter 3

# TABLE TURNERS & PHYSICAL MEDIUMS

If the Bell Witch achieved national fame across the United States, most other early visitations achieved only local notice.

But 1848 saw the beginning of a visitation that would create an international stir. It would dominate discussion of the entire poltergeist phenomenon for more than half a century. The case remains hugely

controversial among researchers. It is best to start with a description of what actually happened before looking at how the visitation and the events that flowed from it were interpreted.

## The Fox Sisters

In 1847 the Fox family moved into a small wooden house in Hydesville, New York State. They planned on living there until their new home in Rochester was available. At the time the family consisted of John Fox, his wife Margaret, ten-year-old Katie and 14-year-old Maggie. An elder brother named David and an elder sister named Leah were living in Rochester. In March 1848, the Fox family began to hear odd noises, which sounded rather like hollow knocks. These were followed by the sounds of furniture being dragged across the wooden floors. Whenever the noises were investigated, there was no explanation to be found. There were no intruders in the house and no furniture had been moved.

The sounds rapidly increased in volume and frequency and for some reason the two girls decided that they were caused by a ghost. They insisted on sleeping in a bed that had been placed in their parents' room. Katie and Maggie started calling the invisible intruder 'Mr Splitfoot', because all of the demons in the books at their school were depicted with cloven hooves. On the night of 31 March the noises had begun just after the family had gone to bed, which was the usual pattern. On this occasion, though, Katie decided to face the unseen visitor. Sitting up in bed she called out, 'Mr Splitfoot, do as I do.' She then clapped her hands. The knocking noises started, but they ended as soon as Katie stopped clapping.

*Three of a kind: the Fox sisters, seen here at the height of their fame, were at the centre of a famous visitation that was to lead to the establishment of spiritualism*

Then it was Maggie's turn to call out, 'Now do just as I do. Count 1, 2, 3, 4.' Maggie clapped her hands four times and she was answered by four knocks.

Mrs Fox decided to take a hand at this point. She asked the invisible knocker to count out the ages of her children. The knocks began again as the phantom presence began to tap out the age of each child. A gap was left between each one. Then after a short pause the ghost added three more thumps. Very few people outside the family knew that Mrs Fox had given birth to a child that had died some years earlier, at the age of three. This convinced Mrs Fox that they were dealing with something that possessed intelligence and knowledge. 'Is this a human being that answers my questions?' she called out. There was silence. 'Is it a spirit?' she asked. And then she added, 'If it is, make two raps.' Instantly there were two loud knocks. Over the following few days the Fox girls and their mother worked out a system by which the spirit could answer their questions. One rap meant 'yes', two raps meant 'no' and other numbers stood for various commonly used words. They later devised a code that enabled the spirit to use letters to spell out some of the more obscure words and names.

The Foxes' neighbours were invited in to witness their conversations with the spirit. Some of them recorded the results. It gradually emerged that the spirit was claiming to be the unquiet soul of Charles B. Rosa, or Rosma, a murdered man. The spirit used both names. Rosa claimed that he had been a pedlar in life – and a successful one at that. He said that when he had come to Hydesville about five years earlier the man who had then lived in the Fox house had offered him accommodation. His host had then slashed his throat in the middle of the night. The foul deed had been done in the bedroom that was later to be occupied by the two girls, said the spirit. That was why the knockings had begun there. The murderer had then stolen his money and his goods before burying his body in the cellar.

Almost as soon as this story had been revealed, a series of new manifestations began. They took the form of a horrific gurgling noise, which was taken to be the sound of the unfortunate Rosa having his throat cut, followed by the sound of a body being dragged over the floor of the bedroom – the scene of the crime. The Foxes and their neighbours went down to the cellar and began digging. They found a few pieces of old bone, but it was never very clear if these were human or not. Then Mrs Fox began asking the locals about pedlars.

She came across a young woman who had worked as a maid in the house five years earlier, when it had been owned by a man named Bell. The woman recalled that one evening Bell had brought a man called Ryan home, who was going to stay the night. She thought he could have been a pedlar. There was no sign of him next morning, so she assumed he had left early.

That seemed to fit in with Rosa's story, apart from the fact that the woman had called him Ryan. Without more ado, Mrs Fox began telling everyone that the spirit's story was true. Bell lived only a few miles away so he was understandably not impressed by the unfolding events. He went to his old home and demanded that the Foxes stop spreading stories about him. They responded that it was the spirit of Rosa who had accused him, not they. Bell then went to the police, who searched their records for any mention of a missing person who had gone by the name of Rosa, Rosma or Ryan. Their best efforts drew a blank. They met with no greater success when they combed the New York State records for missing pedlars.

Although Bell declared himself vindicated, the police still took no action against the Fox family. Thinking there was no smoke without fire, the people of the town began to treat the unfortunate Bell with suspicion and hostility, so he moved away.

Also soon to move were the Fox sisters. As the house in Hydesville became inundated with visitors, sensation-seekers and others, their parents sent them to live with their brother David and their sister Leah in Rochester. The mysterious noises seemed to follow them, because they stopped at Hydesville but broke out in Rochester. When a friend of Leah's came to visit she heard the noises and said she thought it was all a clever trick. An ornament then leapt off a shelf and flew at her head, though it narrowly missed her.

In 1850, Leah suggested that instead of allowing an endless procession of strangers to tramp through her house, they should hire a theatre for a night and invite along everyone who was interested in hearing the mysterious noises. The evening proved to be a great success and it also turned a profit. The girls also discovered that they could communicate with any number of dead spirits, not just the unfortunate Rosa. Leah then suggested that her two younger sisters should put on regular displays.

Before long the Fox girls were touring towns and cities with their show. The knockings and the rappings were now claiming to be the spirits of the dead friends and relatives of people in the audience. The shows became enormously popular and the profits made by the Fox family rose rapidly.

Horace Greeley, a publisher, then became involved. He introduced the Fox sisters to high society and ensured that they got generally favourable coverage in the press. The Quaker community of New York State also took an interest in the girls and many of them became convinced that they really were able to communicate with the dead. By 1855, the girls' activity had become known as 'spiritualism'. All of this sparked off a hot debate, not only among religious leaders but in the whole of society.

If the phenomena were genuine, as many thought, were they caused by spirits, demons or other supernatural beings?

## Table Turning

It was not long before other people began to claim that they could produce similar phenomena to the Fox girls. First of all, the Fox sisters' imitators came up with something that would later go by the name of 'table turning', though table turning was only a part of what happened. According to its followers, table turning could be reproduced successfully in most homes on most occasions. The Fox sisters did not restrict themselves to stage appearances; their audiences could sometimes be relatively small. The method they used on these occasions was copied by the table-turning fraternity. A group of at least four, but no more than 12, adults sat round a table with their hands placed flat on the tabletop, palm side down. The people were then expected to chat amiably amongst

*The publisher Horace Greeley believed that the Fox sisters were producing genuine phenomena and introduced them to leading figures of the day*

themselves – they could even crack jokes – while they called upon the spirits to move the table.

In successful table-turning sessions the table would move about the room. It might even produce knocks or raps, as if it were being hit by a hard object. Most sessions went no further than random movements of the table, together with a few strange knocks. If things got more dramatic the table would levitate or 'dance' with odd jerking movements as it hopped about. A few table turners claimed to be able to talk to the spirits by using a code of rapping or jumping movements. One thing was generally recognized among table turners – for a session to be successful it was necessary for all of those present to believe that the table would move. If even one of the participants expressed scepticism, the manifestations would be weak or absent altogether.

During 1852 and 1853 table turning became a popular parlour game across North America and Europe. But scientists stepped in to denounce the explanation that spirits were involved. Instead, they ascribed the phenomenon to electricity, the rotation of the earth or magnetism. It was the ageing physicist Michael Faraday who came up with a way of scientifically testing the phenomenon. As expected by the table turners, though, the presence of the sceptical Faraday put a damper on things. A few minor table shuffles did take place at one sitting, but Faraday's equipment had detected an involuntary spasm in the arms of one of the sitters just as the table had moved. That was enough for Faraday, who immediately announced that table turning was due to the involuntary movements of the sitters. The scientific world took up Faraday's conclusions and trumpeted them widely. Everyone ignored the fact that Faraday's findings did not explain the levitations, the jumps or the knocks. So far as the press and the scientists were concerned, table turning had been explained away. Despite this setback, it continued to produce some impressive phenomena for those prepared to continue with it.

Some of these people discovered that they had a special gift for producing dramatic results. Not only did the table move but so did other objects in the room – but these results remained unpredictable and unreliable. In time, however, the table-turning practitioners who went down this route devised a procedure that stood a far better chance of producing interesting phenomena – they called it a seance. But that development was not going to come to fruition for another two decades or so. Meanwhile, other events began to catch the popular imagination.

## Physical Mediums

In 1854 an exciting new development took place. The Davenport brothers of Buffalo, New York claimed to be able to produce manifestations that were far more impressive than anything that mere table turning, or even the Fox sisters, could produce. The Davenports went on the stage with their demonstration of bizarre effects. When their show began, the brothers were tied to their chairs. This was a way of showing everyone that they were not able to physically influence any of the phenomena that would be witnessed. Objects would then move about, musical instruments would play and other apparently impossible events would take place.

Meanwhile, another New York State resident claimed the ability to communicate with the spirits. This was 15-year-old Cora Scott, who

*An illustration of the Davenport brothers and their famous cabinet: the scale of the apparent activity has been exaggerated – in reality the men were out of sight for most of the show*

became better known under her married name of Cora Hatch. Cora's abilities started just after the death of her father, when she was 13 years old. She began to fall into trances, during which she would speak in foreign languages or write messages that had apparently come from the spirits of the dead. Later on she seemed to acquire the ability to make contact with deceased experts in the sciences and the arts. She was then able to pass on their knowledge to the world. In view of her lack of knowledge of these subjects, the level of expertise she displayed was truly remarkable.

For some years Cora displayed her abilities to small groups of people who were interested in the emerging cult of spiritualism. However, after her marriage to Benjamin Hatch she followed the Fox sisters and the Davenport brothers on to the stage.

Her public success was enormous. It was no doubt helped by her youth and good looks. As well as appearing on stage, Cora also wrote books while she was in her trances: these sold well. After several years, Cora's gifts began to fade. She was no longer able to enter trances as easily as before, nor were her feats as impressive.

Meanwhile, the Davenports met with disaster when they went on a tour of Europe in 1864. Their show in Paris was watched by the most famous European illusionist and conjurer of the time, Jean Eugène Robert-Houdin. He suspected trickery and he said so. Within a month, Houdin had worked out a method of reproducing the supposedly impossible feats of the Davenports. He put on a stage show in which he replicated the Davenport show and then he explained how it had been done. The performer must first of all have an assistant behind the scenes.

Then he must have the ability to slip out of the knots while he was inside the cabinet or sitting behind the tablecloth.

The Davenports denied that any trickery was involved, but they moved to Britain to continue their tour. Sadly, they came to grief in London. An English stage conjuror who had read about Houdin asked a sailor to show him how to tie a knot that could not be wriggled out of. He then went to the Davenport show in the hope of being called up on stage to test the knots. After several visits he was eventually selected. He used the opportunity to tie the brothers up with his special knot and then he sat back to watch. The Davenports were unable to perform, their secret was unmasked and a near riot followed as the audience demanded their money back. The Davenports later enjoyed a reasonable career as conjurors and illusionists, but they never earned as much as when they had claimed that the spirits were assisting them.

Meanwhile, the seance had come into vogue. People could now produce dramatic manifestations such as knocks, levitations and the movement of objects. In most cases seances produced no more than these physical manifestations. However, some seance leaders claimed the ability to contact spirits – they would later become known as 'mediums'. These mediums might go into trances, during which they claimed to speak with the voices of spirits. At other times, they could interpret knocking sounds as messages or they might write messages on scraps of paper.

By the 1880s a number of people claimed to be gifted mediums, who were able to contact any named spirit almost on demand. They were now charging for their services, often obtaining large sums of money from those who wished to talk to their deceased loved ones. At the same time public interest in table turning and seances was waning. They were no longer popular as parlour games.

As we have seen, the Fox sisters had started the whole spiritualism movement. But in 1888 they made a truly startling announcement: they insisted they had faked the whole thing.

The background to this move by the sisters, now middle-aged women, was complex.

For a start, they were no longer earning much money. The success of their stage show, managed by their elder sister Leah, had long since faded. Added to that, Kate had taken to drink and had become so violently unpredictable that her ex-husband's relatives were starting legal action to have her children taken away from her. Maggie, meanwhile, had suffered a crisis of faith after converting to Catholicism.

First of all, she had abandoned her beliefs and then she had re-embraced them. Finally, after a quarrel with Leah, the sisters went to a newspaper. They offered to come clean about their fraudulent activities in return for a cash sum of $1,500. The newspaper paid up and on 21 October 1888 the confession was made to a packed audience at the New York Academy of Music.

It was Maggie who did all the talking; Kate just sat silently listening. According to Maggie the initial incidents back in Hydesville had begun as a school prank.

> *When we went to bed at night we used to tie an apple to a string and move the string up and down, causing the apple to bump on the floor, or we would drop the apple on the floor, making a strange noise every time it would*

*rebound. Mother listened to this for a time. She would not understand it and did not suspect us as being capable of a trick because we were so young.*

She then went on to explain that the mysterious rappings that had taken place in private meetings and on stage had been faked using a method devised after the girls had moved to Rochester.

*My sister Katie was the first to observe that by swishing her fingers she could produce certain noises with her knuckles and joints, and that the same effect could be made with the toes. Finding that we could make raps without moving our feet – first with one foot and then with both – we practised until we could do this easily when the room was dark. Like most perplexing things when made clear, it is astonishing how easily it is done. The rappings are simply the result of perfect control of the muscles of the leg below the knee, which govern the tendons of the foot and allow action of the toe and ankle bones that is not commonly known. Such perfect control is only possible when the child is taken at an early age and carefully and continually taught to practise the muscles which grow stiffer in later years. This, then, is the simple explanation of the whole method of the knocks and raps.*

She then proceeded to produce a series of sample raps. First she produced them as she would have done in a meeting, with her feet under a table. Then she removed the table cloth and showed the audience how she slipped her shoes off so that her toes would have the necessary space in which to move and produce the noises.

Maggie continued her explanation:

*A great many people when they hear the rapping imagine at once that the spirits are touching them. It is a very common delusion. Some very wealthy people came to see me some years ago when I lived in 42nd Street and I did some rapping for them. I made the spirit rap on the chair and one of the ladies cried out, 'I feel the spirit tapping me on the shoulder.' Of course that was pure imagination.*

Maggie went on to launch a devastating attack on spiritualism and all those who practised table turning or conducted seances. She said the entire movement was a fraud and all of those involved were guilty of trickery and deceit.

Reaction to the public revelation was fiercely divided. Among those present were some who had been present at the original events in Hydesville and others who had seen the Fox sisters in the early days at Rochester. They insisted that the noises that Maggie had produced on stage were nothing like those they had experienced at the time of the disturbances.

They said that the earlier noises had been much louder and had come from different parts of the room, not just from the table. They also claimed that the original noises had been of a different quality or type altogether.

On the other hand, the scientists and the sceptics in the audience hailed the confession as an explanation of the entire affair. They used Maggie's statement to denounce the spiritualist movement and explain away all of the phenomena that emerged at table-turning sessions or seances. So far as science was concerned, the matter was settled.

Kate Fox's reaction was interesting. In letters written after the public confession she denounced her sister for her attacks on spiritualism and spiritualists. She died soon after of an alcohol-related disease. About a year later Maggie recanted her confession. She announced that the original phenomena in Hydesville and Rochester had all been genuine. The later fakery had, she said, been the fault of Leah, who had wanted to maintain the flow of money coming in from the stage show even after the manifestations had faded. Maggie then spoke in support of mediums. She said that their work was as valid and genuine as her early manifestations had been.

The spiritualist movement, as it had become, continued in a low-key fashion over the next two decades. Scientists tended to ignore it and most of the public treated it as an interesting curiosity that had neither been proved nor disproved. So things might have continued had it not been for the outbreak of the First World War.

During the four years of carnage on the Western Front, millions of men were killed. Fathers, sons and husbands were slaughtered in huge numbers. Before 1914, soldiering had been viewed as a reliable career for anyone who chose it, but most men were not called upon to face the horrors of war. Suddenly ordinary men were marched off to face the enemy. So many were lost in battle that there was a massive public reaction.

At first, the First World War had a beneficial effect on spiritualism. Large numbers of the bereaved sought solace from their grief in the belief that their dead relatives had passed over to a better place. Many rediscovered their faith in Christianity, but others turned to mediums in the hope of making direct contact with their lost ones. Those mediums and spiritualists who had continued with their work after the Fox confessions found themselves inundated with demands for assistance. Soon, large numbers of new mediums appeared on the scene, all offering to help people communicate with the dead soldiers. Bereaved relatives flocked to the mediums, some of whom charged high prices for entry to their seances. The more accomplished mediums produced truly dramatic effects. Ghosts walked the rooms, voices spoke and disembodied hands appeared to move objects about.

## Denouncing the Fakes

It looked as if spiritualism was on the rise, but some viewed the developments with scepticism. The high earnings of some of the more dramatic mediums aroused suspicions. Harry Houdini was among those who were disinclined to believe in the reality of what was going on. Houdini had taken his stage name from Jean Eugène Robert-Houdin, who had been instrumental in unmasking the Davenport brothers.

While Houdini is best known for his dramatic feats of escapology, he was also a gifted illusionist and stage conjurer. He attended a few seances after his mother died and became quickly convinced that trickery was involved. As a result, he spent some time devising ways in which he could replicate the manifestations that he had seen. Then he practised the tricks until he was certain that he was correct.

His next task was to consult various lawyers in order to establish whether these mediums could be taken to task. He was informed that

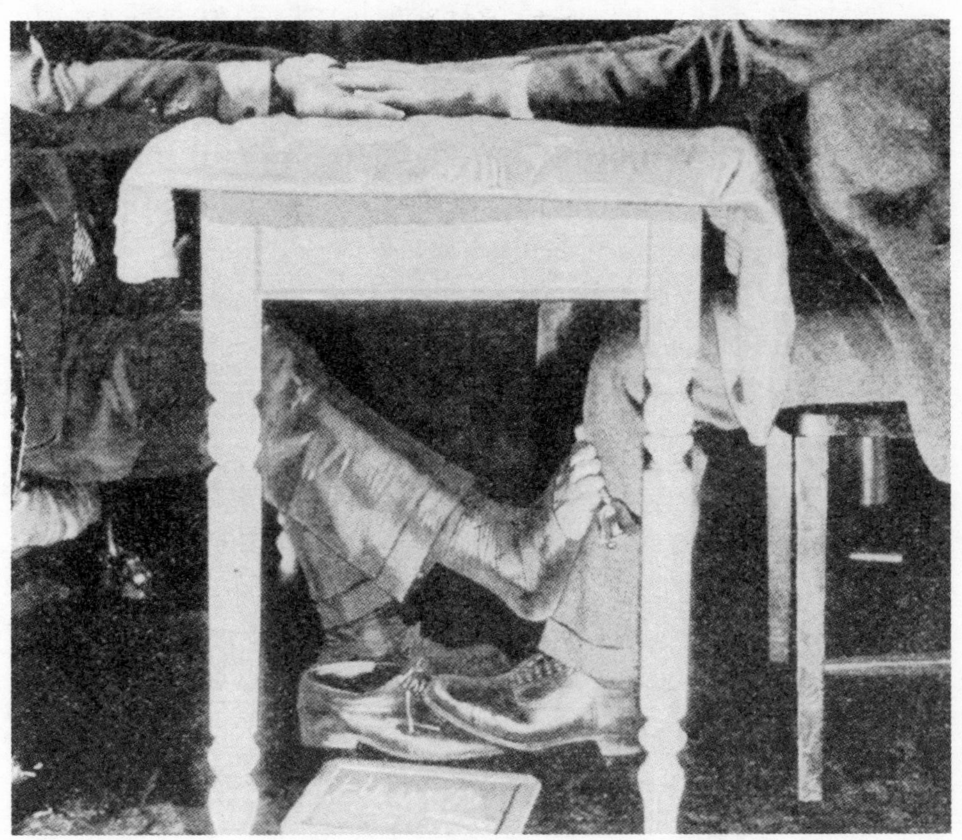

*A fake medium could ring a bell and fake a handgrip under the table while his own hands were securely held. Such simple trickery could be surprisingly effective in dimly lit rooms*

they would be guilty of fraud if they took money after falsely claiming to be able to contact the dead. Houdini began a systematic campaign of unmasking the heartless mediums who charged the bereaved exorbitant fees for attending their seances. After booking himself into sessions under an assumed name, he attended with a newspaper reporter and a police officer. The campaigner waited until he was certain that he knew how the 'medium' was performing the trick – then he would stand up and declare his real name. He would first announce how the trick was done and then he would go on to reveal the fraudulent devices and mechanisms that were being used. Finally, the policeman would arrest the medium while the reporter took notes. Houdini would later exploit his success by going on stage to replicate the stunts that he had unmasked. Amazingly, some of the discredited 'mediums' appeared with him.

Houdini's campaign against Mina Crandon, or 'Margery', turned out to be both spectacular and contentious. It began in 1924, when she claimed a prize of $2,500 from the magazine *Scientific American*. The magazine had offered the reward to anyone who could convince their committee that they were able to produce 'physical manifestations of a psychic nature under scientific control'. The manifestations produced by Margery were impressive and no evidence of trickery was found. Convinced at last, the committee was on the point of declaring for Margery and awarding her the prize. But Houdini had just published a book based on his anti-medium campaign. Armed with his expert knowledge, he decided to take a hand.

The events that followed were controversial. Houdini decided to submit Margery's claim to a series of tests. They involved asking Margery

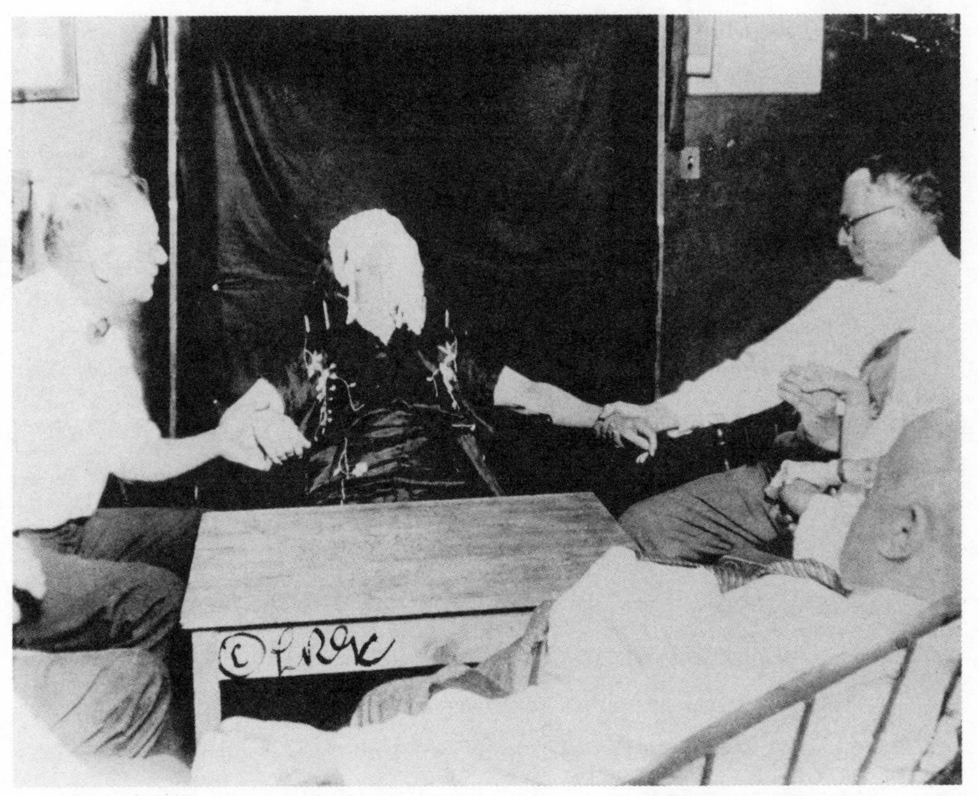

*This sceance shows what purports to be ectoplasm issuing from a medium's face. In most cases, 'ectoplasm' turned out to be muslin or some other cloth*

to reproduce the effects she had achieved in her seances, but using equipment supplied by Houdini. There were several minor incidents, but nothing on the scale that she usually achieved. Margery accused Houdini of making it impossible for her to succeed by sabotaging her equipment. Houdini denied the charge. He claimed that Margery had tampered with the mechanism herself in order to provide an excuse for failure. A second round of tests was arranged, but in the meantime a sceptic attending one of Margery's routine seances had witnessed one of her tricks. By gripping a long dark rod in her mouth she had been able to manipulate objects on a table. *Scientific American* decided that Margery had failed the test.

All of this had been played out in the full glare of publicity. Houdini's campaign, and the activities of other sceptics, resulted in numerous 'mediums' being exposed. Several of these tricksters were prosecuted for having obtained money under false pretences. This effectively destroyed the credibility of the physical mediums – that is, those who produced knocks and raps or moved objects around during seances. Interestingly, one of those who played a minor role in the denouncing of fake mediums was an amateur historian named Harry Price. Price would later go on to lead a colourful and rather controversial life as an investigator of the paranormal. He would be called in to deal with several poltergeist cases and his work would become instrumental in defining and categorizing different types of haunting.

Table turning had already been dismissed as a fad – now the holding of seances disappeared as a pastime as well. Thereafter seances and the like retreated to the world of fiction. They either became the stuff of horror stories or they were treated with comical contempt. Physical

*Scourge of the phoney spiritualists, Harry Houdini poses for a deliberately fake spirit photograph in order to demonstrate how the forgeries were produced. Fake photos of spirits were hugely popular until the trickery involved was revealed to the public*

mediumship was then abandoned by the spiritualist movement. The practice and the beliefs that surrounded the movement had developed in a number of different ways, one of which was the founding of spiritualist churches. However, when physical phenomena were no longer a part of the discipline the relevance of the movement to the study of poltergeists vanished.

## Where Does This Leave Poltergeists?

Looking back at these events from the early 21st century, some things are clear that were not so obvious at the time. Contemporary accounts of the original experience of the Fox sisters at Hydesville read very much like those of other early visitations. The disturbances began fairly quietly with some odd noises in the girls' bedroom. Then the noises became louder and more insistent: the girls decided that they were caused by a ghost. When whatever it was began to communicate through coded rappings it announced that it was a ghost. So it was fitting in with the expectations of the viewer. Not only that but the ghost was not the phantom of some boringly normal inhabitant of Hydesville, but that of an exotic pedlar. And he had been murdered as well. Finally, when the Fox girls moved to Rochester, the noises went with them. It all sounds very familiar. Read in isolation, the experiences of the Fox sisters might be viewed as a typical poltergeist visitation.

It is what happened next that is unusual. Unlike most recipients of the attentions of a poltergeist, the Fox sisters did not find it troublesome – in fact, they welcomed its activities. They then went on to invite people round to witness the manifestations. When the 'ghost' had an audience it accused a local man of murder, which led to quite a degree of fuss and resentment. This is reminiscent of the behaviour of the Cock Lane Ghost. However, when the Fox sisters went on stage and started to earn money from the phenomena that surrounded them it was something that had never happened before. Those who saw the stage act were divided. Some thought it was genuine, others imagined that the girls were involved in trickery. Again, it might be useful to compare the Fox sisters' case with that of the Cock Lane Ghost. In the latter instance, the phenomena were on the wane when the start of a court case put pressure on the ghost to perform. That was when Elizabeth Parsons was caught cheating. Similarly, it was when the Fox girls were earning considerable sums of money that they were suspected of trickery.

Maggie Fox's later confession is an interesting matter. Once again, she was offered money, but this time it was to denounce the supernatural elements of her story. Her account of how she and her sister created rapping and knocking noises is quite obviously true in the context of the later years of the girls' stage careers. Those who had not known the girls at Hydesville soon believed, therefore, that the entire phenomenon had been a fraud. But those who had experienced the earlier manifestations were not convinced. They maintained that the earlier noises had been louder and different. At a later date, when the financial pressure was off, Maggie took back her confession. She said the original events had been genuine.

In the case of the Fox sisters, the most reasonable interpretation of events would be that a real poltergeist – whatever that might be – had initially been involved. Maggie's later confession does not really ring true. It is hard to imagine how the bouncing of an apple on a wooden floor could be mistaken for loud bangs.

In any case, many of the noises occurred when both girls were in the room. It would have been clear that they were not bouncing apples about. And how was it that the girls were too young to have been suspected of trickery? As we have seen, Maggie was 14 years old at the time and her sister was ten. If they had been three or four years old the comment might have made sense, but teenagers are notoriously prone to fibbing and pranks.

It is noticeable that Maggie remained vague about the later phenomena in her recantation. By the time of her confession many of her friends were mediums, or were otherwise involved with spiritualism. Understandably, she became alienated from them because of her denunciation of their activities. Perhaps she wanted to regain their friendship.

That raises the issue of the mediums and spiritualists who followed the Fox sisters' lead. Some were undoubtedly fraudulent, such as the Davenport brothers. However, others might have actually believed that they were creating phenomena when the cause of their psychic powers was more down to earth. For example, young Cora Hatch might have been genuinely declaiming knowledge quite beyond anything she possessed in her normal state. There is no reason to ascribe this to spirits, though. She might just have been recalling things she had heard many years earlier, which her conscious mind had forgotten. Hypnotists recognize that those in a trance can recall the details of a past event much more clearly and easily than they do when they are awake.

The phenomena experienced at table-turning sessions and some seances are rather more interesting. Happenings like the sound of knuckle raps and the levitation of tables and small ornaments have often been associated with poltergeists. The actions of many poltergeists are, of course, much more dramatic than this. However, the events that were reported at 19th-century seances are very reminiscent of the low-key activities of poltergeists. Unlike the later physical mediums, the table turners were not making money out of their activities, nor were they convincingly shown to be faking.

It was when the 'mediums' moved beyond traditional poltergeist behaviour that they were found to be frauds. The ability to speak to the spirit of a known dead person is not something that is generally associated with poltergeist cases. Poltergeists will usually claim to be the spirit of a person nobody has ever heard of. If they say they are the soul of a real person, it is often a person who died so long ago that nobody is around who can remember them clearly. Or again, as in the Cock Lane Ghost affair, the claim to be a real person is a false claim. Nor does a poltergeist visitation normally involve the sighting of ghosts. Apparitions tend to be vague, temporary, almost shapeless and usually black. Human figures clad in white, diaphanous robes appeared at seances held by mediums, but they are not associated with poltergeists.

With only the accounts left by 19th-century table turners and attendees at seances to work with, it is impossible to be certain. However, it does seem that some of the low-key phenomena were genuine, at least in the sense that the people involved did not cause them. Similarly, the more dramatic instances of physical mediumship can probably be discounted as clever conjuring tricks by people intent on making money out of the bereaved. It appears that the entire spiritualist saga had been something of a blind alley for those investigating hauntings and poltergeists. As we shall see in a later chapter, however, the events that followed the Fox sisters' experiences might actually hold the key to unlocking the poltergeist mystery.

Meanwhile, the events at Hydesville, and in seance rooms around the world, did have one important and lasting effect. They convinced the scientific establishment that the entire poltergeist phenomenon was a nonsense that was not worth investigating. In earlier years poltergeist visitations had often attracted educated gentlemen or clergymen who were interested in observing and recording what happened. For some time after the Fox sisters' experiences this ceased to be the case. Many of the visitations that took place over the following years were effectively ignored and not recorded properly. As far as the majority of scientists are concerned, things have not moved on at all. Poltergeists and the manifestations they produce are not real, according to conventional science. It was not until the later 20th century that a few scientists began to break ranks by being prepared to treat the subject seriously.

The general public, on the other hand, came to a rather different conclusion. They came to believe that any strange events of the poltergeist type were the work of ghosts or spirits. It is to some of those cases that we must now turn.

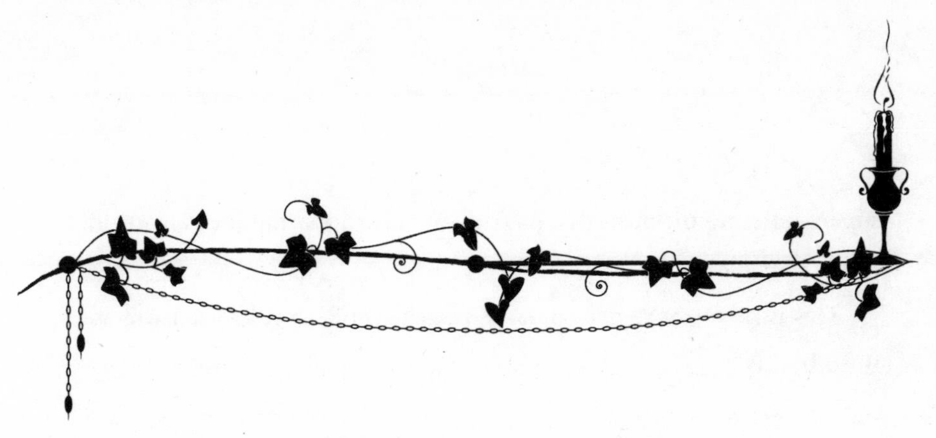

# chapter 4

# CLASSIC VICTORIAN HAUNTINGS

Neither the furore over the Fox sisters and their experiences nor the growth of spiritualism seemed to have much effect on the frequency of poltergeist visitation or the forms that it took.

As with some of the earlier cases, the records that we have are somewhat scanty and incomplete. They often centre on the apparently

supernatural occurrences that took place while ignoring the background to the phenomenon.

This is perfectly understandable, but the modern researcher can find it frustrating.

## The Great Amherst Mystery

But not all of the cases that were reported after the time of the Fox sisters are so fragmentary. Take, for instance, the events that took place in Amherst, Nova Scotia from 1878 to 1879. They would become known as the Great Amherst Mystery. While the visitation was going on the writer Walter Hubbell spent some time in the affected house. He went there with the avowed aim of writing up the 'haunting' in book form, so that it could be published. Some have thought that Hubbell's aim of making money gave him a motive to exaggerate the tale, but whenever the book can be cross-referenced to other contemporary sources its contents seem to be genuine.

The affected house was a relatively small one. It was occupied by Daniel and Olive Teed and their two sons, George and Willie. Also in the house were Olive's two younger sisters, Jennie and Esther Cox, plus her brother William. Daniel's brother John also lived in the fairly crowded house. When he came to investigate the 'haunting', Hubbell thought it was significant that Jennie, aged 22, was very pretty but that Esther, aged 18, was considered plain. Despite this, Esther was the one with a long-term boyfriend. He was called Bob MacNeal and he was known locally as a bit of a tough who was suspected of some petty pilfering.

In August 1878 Daniel Teed's cow stopped giving the usual amount of milk. He suspected that somebody had been milking the cow surreptitiously. Esther loved drinking milk so he imagined that either she or her boyfriend were to blame. A few days later Bob MacNeal packed his bags, abandoned his lodgings and left Amherst without leaving any forwarding address. Esther was understandably distraught. The visitation began one week later.

On the evening of 4 September, Esther climbed into her bed in the room that she shared with Jennie. Almost at once she screamed and leapt out again, saying that there was a mouse in the bed. Jennie stripped the bed, but could find no sign of any mouse. On the following evening, both girls heard what sounded like a mouse scurrying about under Esther's bed. Jennie peered under the bed and spotted a small cardboard box. The box suddenly moved so Jennie thought that the mouse must be inside it.

She pulled the box out so that it stood in the middle of the floor. The box gave a sudden jerk and fell over. But when the lid fell open the girls could see that there was nothing there. They set the box upright again and once more it flipped over. Daniel Teed came in at this point. He told them that they were imagining things and ordered them to bed.

On the following evening, Esther complained that she felt unwell. She went to bed early but a few minutes later she was heard screaming. Jennie ran to see what was wrong. When she got there Esther's face was flushed bright red and her hair was standing on end. Then her body began to swell up. Jennie called for Daniel, who dashed in with John and William. At that moment there was a terrific bang, as if somebody had fired a cannon just outside the house. The men ran outside, found nothing and came back indoors. Esther was fast asleep and her appearance was normal.

Two nights later Esther felt ill again. This time Jennie accompanied her to the bedroom and saw her face turn red for herself. She called for the men, who came in just as the bedclothes flew off Esther's bed. They drifted through the air to collapse in a pile in the corner. When John went over to look at them, a pillow rose into the air and hovered for a moment before hitting him hard on the head. He immediately fled. On the following day he sent a message asking for his clothes to be sent to a nearby boarding house, where he had taken up residence. He never returned to the house. After John had left the invisible cannon fired again, twice this time. Again Esther collapsed into sleep and once more her appearance returned to normal.

Daniel Teed summoned Dr Carritte as soon as he could. The doctor could find nothing wrong with Esther, but as he finished his inspection the girl's pillow flew across the room. Dr Carritte put it back, but again it left the bed and hurtled through the air. Then a scratching noise began to be heard. It was apparently coming from inside the wall above Esther's bed. As the appalled doctor watched, scratch marks began to appear on the wall as if made by an invisible claw. The marks gradually became more controlled until they took the form of writing. The words could be clearly seen: 'Esther Cox, you are mine to kill.' This was followed by a series of knocks and bangs that continued for two hours.

Over the following three weeks, the knocking noises gradually increased in frequency and volume. They were especially loud on the day after Dr Carritte had given Esther a dose of morphine to help her sleep.

Then Esther broke down and told the doctor and her sister that there was more to Bob MacNeal's sudden departure than met the eye. On the day before he left she had been out for a drive in the country with him in a borrowed pony and trap. Once they had reached a remote spot, Bob had tried to persuade her to have sex with him. When she refused he pulled out a gun and seemed intent on raping her. A farm cart had then lumbered into view and Bob had fled.

Jennie started to blame Bob MacNeal for the haunting. Her words were followed by a very loud thump on the wall. Dr Carritte remarked that the 'ghost' seemed to understand everything they said. He was rewarded with three distinct knocks. The doctor then decided to ask the ghost some questions. He suggested that one knock should mean 'no', two knocks should signify 'do not know' and three knocks should stand for 'yes'. There came three knocks as if the ghost were agreeing, but the subsequent question and answer session made no sense at all.

The knocking noises continued for some weeks. They became so loud that they could be heard from outside the house. A crowd often gathered to listen. In December Esther fell ill with diphtheria and the manifestations stopped. She went away to stay with relatives while she recuperated and during that time there were no disturbances, either in Amherst or at her temporary home. They began again when she returned to Amherst. Soon after she got home, Esther called the rest of the family into her room. She said that a disembodied voice had announced that the house was going to be set on fire. At that instant a lit match appeared out of thin air and dropped on to Esther's bed. Jennie put it out. Another match fell and was put out. Then over a dozen lit matches materialized at various points around the room. They all fell to the floor. And then the knocking noises began again.

Over the next week several small fires broke out. The first fire left one of Esther's dresses smouldering while a second set a barrel of tinder ablaze. The family's neighbours were alarmed by the fires because all of the houses in the town were built of wood, so they demanded that Esther be sent away. A restaurant owner in the town named John White thought this was uncharitable, so he offered Esther a live-in job. Nothing happened during the first two weeks of Esther's new job. Then one day, as she was scrubbing the floor, the brush leapt out of her hand and floated up to the ceiling. It hovered there for several seconds before dropping. On the following day the oven door flung itself open repeatedly. Then Esther seemed to become a powerful magnet. Cutlery and other objects would fly across the room to stick to her. One knife cut her as it made contact and she bled profusely.

White thought that an excess of electricity might be to blame. He had a pair of shoes with insulated soles made and he asked Esther to wear them. The magnetic activity ended but Esther developed severe headaches and bad nosebleeds, so she refused to wear the shoes. However, the magnetism did not return. Instead the wooden furniture in the restaurant began to slide about of its own accord. This began to put customers off, so White reluctantly told Esther she had to go home. In fact, Esther went to stay with an elder sister who was married to a farmer near New Brunswick. As before, the manifestations ceased while she was away – though Esther said she began to hear voices when she was alone. When she returned to Amherst in June 1879 the visitation began again. This was the point at

*Supernatural target practice: one day metal objects flew at Esther Cox as if she were a powerful magnet. The effect lasted for several days, but stopped when she began wearing insulated shoes*

which Hubbell took an interest. He wrote and asked if he could come to stay in the 'haunted house' as a paying guest. Daniel Teed agreed so Hubbell moved in.

The writer had been in the house for less than five minutes when his umbrella rose from the corner where he had left it and floated across the room to fall at his feet. Undeterred, he sat down to talk to Teed, whereupon a nearby chair lurched across the room and banged into his. Esther then came in from her bedroom, where she had been resting. She said that the spirit voices had told her that Hubbell was unwelcome. Hubbell said he had come to stay and he was not leaving. At that, all the chairs in the room started to hop and dance about. The visitation seemed to escalate rapidly over the next few days, as if Hubbell was indeed resented. No fewer than 45 small fires broke out, Esther was stabbed by pins on 30 different occasions and small objects floated around the house more than ever before. But Hubbell persisted. He eventually persuaded the spirits to communicate with him by using a code of raps. The more dramatic activity then tailed off.

The spirits refused to talk about themselves, so Hubbell was unable to discover anything as to their origin or their motives. He did, however, get them to tell him what they would do next – things like moving a chair or floating an ornament around the room. They also told him what he had written down and they even knew the dates on the coins in his pocket. Hubbell visited the Amherst house several times over the following months. He closely questioned witnesses about the events that had occurred before he arrived and then he interacted with the spirits and watched the manifestations, which were always at their strongest when Esther was having her periods, he noticed. He linked this to the fact that the visitation had begun just after the attempted rape. However, he was unable to formulate a theory as to quite how these features were all connected. After collecting all the evidence that he needed for his book, Hubbell suggested that the afflicted household might earn some money by putting Esther on the stage. Perhaps she could get her spirits to perform in public, as the Fox sisters had done. The enterprise proved a failure, because the spirits never turned up. In any case the visitation seemed to be winding down – the incidents were not as frequent and they were becoming less severe.

After a few months of peace, Esther left home to take a job on a farm run by a couple named Davidson. Soon after she arrived, the Davidsons' neighbours reported a series of petty thefts. The stolen objects were found in the Davidsons' barn. Mr Davidson suspected Esther but he was uncertain if he should report the matter. Then his barn burned down and Esther was thrown into prison, accused of arson and theft. She was released after four months. It was never entirely clear if the fire had been caused by Esther, by accident or by the 'spirits'. Whatever the truth the visitation was very definitely over by the time Esther left prison. She went on to lead a conventional and entirely blameless life.

## The Fowler Visitation

Another well-documented, late-19th-century case took place in a house near the village of Appleby in what was then Westmorland, but is now Cumbria. One of those involved kept a diary and wrote down the events as they happened, allowing us to follow the progress of this particular visitation in detail.

The house in question was a former flour mill which, like so many in England, was abandoned in the 1880s when cheap grain was imported from North America and milled at the dockside. In 1887 the semi-derelict old watermill was bought by a businessman from Manchester named Fowler. His plan was to turn it into a comfortable country home for his family, which consisted of his wife and two daughters – Teddie aged 12 and Jessica aged 14. After he had moved his family in, Fowler would have to spend part of his time in Manchester. He intended to occupy a small apartment over his business when he did so. But the old mill had to be converted into a home before the family could move in.

Most of the changes were cosmetic, but one modification was more substantial than the others. It was to have a huge impact on the lives of the mill's occupants. The mill's water wheel had formerly been linked to a large axle that had entered the mill through the side wall overlooking the river. After entering the 'wheel room' the axle had been connected to the mass of cogs and gears that powered the milling machinery. The room was lit by a large window, while a door gave access to some stone steps and a gantry from which the water wheel could be inspected and repaired. A door led from the wheel room into the kitchen.

Fowler hired a gang of workmen to remove the wheel and all of the machinery. He then had the door bricked up, but he left the window as it was. The wall separating the wheel room from the kitchen was torn down and replaced by a flimsy partition that stood much closer to the outside wall.

This created a far larger kitchen that now had the advantage of a window overlooking the river. A storeroom now occupied the greatly reduced wheel room – but the family still called it the wheel room. The building work was finished in early May 1887 and the family moved in. About two weeks later, Teddie complained of feeling ill. When she began to run a slight fever her mother put her to bed and decided that she should rest there for a day or two. That evening the other three members of the family were eating supper in the kitchen when the sound of breaking glass came from the wheel room.

Mr Fowler went into the room to find that a pane of glass in the window had been smashed. At first he thought that a large bird must have flown into the window and broken it, but he soon decided that the pane had been smashed deliberately. He peered out but he could see nobody, so he walked through the kitchen and out into his garden. From this vantage point he could see the stream in both directions and the path that ran along the far side. Again, nobody was in sight. Fowler then returned to the wheel room and began clearing up the broken glass. He quickly found the missile that had smashed the window. It was a large stone, identical to those found in the rocky bed of the stream, and it was still wet. Fowler put the incident down to stray vandals and returned to his family.

Ten days later the family were again at supper in the kitchen when they began to hear the sound of somebody knocking on the far side of the partition. The knocking noises got louder and more insistent and then moved to the door that led from the kitchen into the storage room. Thinking that some prankster was at work, Foster walked over and opened the door. The noises stopped at once. When Foster looked round the room there was nobody there. Three days later Mrs Fowler and Jessica were working in the kitchen when they heard voices coming from the wheel room. The voices were not loud and neither Mrs Fowler nor Jessica could catch what they were saying. They knew that nobody was in the wheel room, and so they fled the house. While they were standing in the garden wondering what to do a man who worked on a neighbouring farm came walking down the lane. Mrs Fowler told the man that she was worried that somebody was in the house. The farmhand went in and searched diligently but found nobody.

That night the voices in the wheel room started again while the family were at supper. This time they were louder. The family could tell that a man and a woman were speaking, though they could not understand what they were saying. Then there came a sound like a saucer falling to the floor and breaking. Mr Fowler quickly opened the door to the room. The voices stopped. There was no broken saucer, nor anything that could have explained the noise. Worrying as the events were, the time had come when Mr Fowler needed to go to Manchester to look after his business. He would be leaving on the following Monday and he would have to stay in Manchester for several days. Although he did not want to leave his family alone, he dreaded what would happen if he announced that the house was haunted. His solution was to sent for an employee named Dick Carter, whom he knew to be level-headed. Carter and his wife would stay at the mill in his absence.

Before Carter arrived, Fowler screwed two stout metal bars across the door that led from the kitchen to the wheel room, so that it could not be opened from either side. As he did so a stone smashed through the window and landed in the wheel room. Fowler then fixed a wire mesh over the outside of the window. On the Monday, Fowler told Carter what had been going on. He expressed his fear that the house was haunted. Carter promised to keep a close eye on things and Foster then left for Manchester.

That evening the people gathered in the kitchen comprised Mr and Mrs Carter, Mrs Fowler, Teddie and Jessica. The two women were clearing up when the manifestations began. This time they were far more dramatic than before. It all began when a cup fell off the dresser, followed by a pair of saucers and another cup. Then a jug of beer tipped over and spilled its contents all over the floor. This was followed by the fire irons, which began dancing about in their holder. Finally, pieces of coal started flying out of the coal scuttle. The girls screamed and dived for cover, followed quickly by Mrs Fowler. But Carter stood up and surveyed the mayhem around him. He had promised to keep an eye on things, so he was determined to remember everything that happened. His employer would expect a report. Suddenly, everything fell still. But not for long.

Noises started to come from the sealed-up wheel room. At first it sounded as if the boxes in the wheel room were being thrown about but then came the sound of hammering and banging. Carter ushered everyone out of the house before getting into a small boat and crossing to the far side of the river. He wanted to get a good view of the wheel room window. He watched as packing cases moved back and forth. Then an empty pram floated up to the ceiling before moving off to one side. The pram drifted past the window five times and then the movements and noises ceased. After 20 minutes of silence, Carter rowed back across the stream and entered the house. All was quiet, so he waved the others in. Carter sat up all night in the kitchen while the others went to bed. There were no more incidents, so he was able to doze off.

Next morning, he climbed up a ladder and peered into the wheel room. All of the packing boxes had been piled up against one wall and the pram was perched on top.

Nothing happened for the rest of the week, but when Fowler came home the disturbances broke out again. Once more the packing cases and the pram were moved around the sealed room and loud hammering noises were heard. Then the voices came back. It sounded as if the man and the woman were having an argument, but as before the actual words could not be distinguished. This lasted for an hour and then quiet returned. Over the months that followed the disturbances continued unabated. There might be a few days when nothing happened, but then the noises and the movements would come back. Mr Fowler's diary entries for a few weeks in August/September are typical. The references to everyday life have been omitted, but the entries that describe the visitation read as follows:

**Saturday, August 13**

*Four jugs broken in kitchen. Several knocks on door. Scraping sound on wheel room window.*

**Monday, August 15**

*Cat frightened at something in kitchen, and has run away.*

**Thursday, August 18**

*Five spoons found on floor of kitchen this morning, on dresser over night. Jess had a plate thrown at her. Noises in the wheel room.*

**Sunday, August 21**

*Quiet, except for jug of water upset, and knives found in sink.*

**Friday, August 26**

*A noisy night last night. On guard outside wheel room. They kept it up for nearly two hours. Ink bottles thrown to floor.*

**Monday, September 5**

*No sleep last night. On guard all night. Hell is in the wheel room. Wife stayed up part of time.*

It is hardly surprising that the Fowler family wanted to take a holiday after such a summer. Mr Fowler's married sister lived on the Isle of Man and he arranged for them all to visit her for a couple of weeks in September. Before leaving he made a point of putting all the loose objects away. Then he made a careful note of where everything was before locking every door. Finally, he asked a neighbour to keep an eye on the place. They agreed to make a daily check on the outside doors and windows.

In the event, the Fowlers were away for four weeks. When the time came to return home, Teddie asked if she could stay on with her aunt. So Mr and Mrs Fowler and Jessica returned without her. The house was exactly as they had left it. There were no further manifestations of any kind.

Once the trouble was over, Fowler felt more inclined to talk about the events. He spoke to the local curate, who agreed to do some research. The curate discovered that one of the former workers at the mill had been a Welshman named Tom Watkins. Watkins had been employed to look after the machinery in the wheel room. He often slept in the room when the mill was busy. When the Welshman had formed a friendship with a local woman, the woman's husband had taken exception to the way in which the 'friendship' was progressing. One night a fight had broken out between Watkins and the husband in the local inn. It had ended with the woman's husband dying from a blow to the head. Watkins was arrested, but he was released after it became clear that the other man had attacked him first. Watkins and the widow then moved off to Wales.

Their subsequent fate was unknown. The visitation was promptly put down to a haunting that was connected to these events. The ghosts that had been heard arguing in the wheel room were assumed to be those of Watkins and his lover.

## The Dagg Farm Visitation

Two years later a farm in Canada became the target of a visitation. Once again the events were carefully recorded by one of the protagonists. The farm was owned by George Dagg, who lived there with his wife Susan, his four-year-old daughter Mary and his two-year-old son Johnny. Also living at the farm was a teenage boy named Dean, who had been hired as an odd job boy, and an 11-year-old orphan named Dinah McLean, whom the Daggs had taken in.

On 15 September 1889, Dean found a $5 bill on the floor. He gave it to Mr Dagg, who recognized it as one of the two notes that he had put into his private bureau on the previous day. When he went to put it back he found that the other note was missing as well. After this note turned up in Dean's room Dagg suspected the boy of theft. But he decided to say nothing – the boy had turned in one note and so might have got cold feet about the attempted crime. That afternoon Mrs Dagg discovered that a piece of human excrement had been smeared across the floor. Because it had happened so soon after the note incident, the event was blamed on Dean. Dagg forced him to clean up the mess and then dragged him off to the nearby town to see the magistrate. Three more streaks of excrement appeared while they were gone, so Dean was clearly not to blame.

The mysterious phenomena escalated rapidly, both in number and intensity. Apart from the disgusting streaks, which continued to appear for a few days, stones began to be thrown. The missiles not only smashed a number of windows but they also hit young Mary. Then food began to be moved about in the dairy, particularly butter.

Several small fires started around the house, which had to be put out, and then pools of water formed on the floor, which had to be mopped up. Within a few days the manifestations began to centre on Dinah. Her lovely long hair, which she wore in a plait, came in for a lot of tugging and pulling. One particular tug was so violent that the plait was almost severed, which forced Dinah to have her hair cut short. Then Dinah claimed that she could hear a voice muttering softly. The others could not hear it at first, but within a day or two they too could hear a gruff male voice. When words could be distinguished they were obscene swear words.

It was at this point that a local man named Woodcock came to the Dagg farm. He asked if he could stay with them while he investigated the haunting. George Dagg agreed to the arrangement. Woodcock wanted to start with the most recent phenomenon so Dinah told him that she had seen something moving in the woodshed. She led Woodcock to the shed, but nothing seemed to be amiss.

Then Dinah called out, 'Are you there, mister?'

This prompted the disembodied voice to reply with a stream of swear words.

When the voice fell silent, Woodcock asked, 'Who are you?'

'I am the Devil,' came the gruff voice. 'I'll have you in my clutches. Get out of this or I'll break your neck.' It then poured out a new torrent of obscenities.

Woodcock sent Dinah to fetch George Dagg while he continued to talk to the voice, which merely swore at him rather than making any meaningful replies. When Dagg arrived in the woodshed, he asked a perfectly understandable question: 'Why on earth have you been bothering me and my family?'

'Just for fun,' came the reply.

'There is no fun in throwing a stone at young Mary,' protested Dagg.

'Poor wee Mary,' exclaimed the voice. 'I did not intend to hit her. I intended it for Dinah. But I did not let the stone hurt her.' More obscenities followed. Then the voice apologized for the fires.

Woodcock stayed on the Dagg farm for several days, during which time the poltergeist activity continued unabated. On one occasion the two younger children claimed that they had seen the ghost. They said it looked like a thin man with a cow's head, complete with horns.

Woodcock tried to get the spirit to communicate in writing, thinking that this would be better evidence than his own notes. The spirit happily picked up a pencil and wrote furiously on a piece of paper. When Woodcock bent over to read what had been written, he saw that it was another stream of swear words. He complained, whereupon the voice said, 'I will steal your pencil.'

The pencil then lifted into the air and flew out of the door. On the following Saturday the voice said that it had decided to leave the Dagg farm the next day. Word got out and early next morning neighbours and friends started arriving. As each one entered, the voice cracked jokes or made amusing comments about the person. It showed a quite astonishing level of knowledge about the locals and their lives. After a while one person, probably Woodcock, remarked that the voice was no longer swearing.

'I am not the person who used the filthy language,' the voice declared. 'I am an angel from Heaven sent by God to drive away that fellow.'

Woodcock pointed out that the voice sounded exactly the same as before, whereupon the voice swore profusely before returning to its humorous remarks. The voice later claimed to be the ghost of a local person who had died about 20 years earlier at the age of 80. Later in the afternoon, the voice changed from being gruff and male to being soft and feminine. It began to sing hymns and said that it would be leaving soon. The fairly substantial crowd that had been questioning it objected and asked it to stay. At 3am the voice said that it really had to leave, but that it would visit the children once more before it left for good. Then it fell silent.

The next morning Mary, Johnny and Dinah came running excitedly into the house. They said they had seen 'a man with a beautiful face and long white hair dressed all in white' in the farmyard. The figure had bent down to cuddle Mary and Johnny while Dinah watched. He had called Johnny 'a fine little fellow' and then he had lifted him up. The man had then let the children go and had smiled at them. Then he had floated gently up into the air, heading upwards as if to heaven, before vanishing. The visitation was over.

## The Haunting of Ballechin House

By the 1890s attitudes toward poltergeist activity had begun to improve. The events surrounding the Fox sisters at Hydesville had faded from memory. Once again reputable people were open to the idea that there were still unexplained phenomena taking place that needed to be investigated. As yet nobody had coined the word 'poltergeist' but a similarity between some cases of hauntings was beginning to be seen.

The activities surrounding Ballechin House near Dunkeld in Perthshire constitute a typical instance from this transitional period. In the 1890s the house was owned by a Captain JMS Steuart, who rented it out, together with the extensive grouse shoot that went with it. In 1896 the house and the shoot were let for a year to a Spanish nobleman, who moved in with his family in time for the grouse season to begin. The nobleman, who preferred to remain anonymous, invited several British friends to spend time at the house. He also hired local staff to run the house, though he brought his own personal servants from Spain. Finally he hired an English butler named Harold Sanders.

The haunting of Ballechin House began as soon as the Spanish family moved in. After 11 weeks of mayhem the Spanish family fled. The events were witnessed by many of the British guests, some of whom were very well connected socially, and the story spread rapidly. Some of the rumours were extremely lurid – they lost nothing in the telling as they passed from person to person. In the end the butler, Harold Sanders, contacted *The Times* newspaper in an attempt to set the record straight. Sanders was the soul of discretion, so he mentioned no names and identified people only by their initials. Presumably this allowed those in the know to identify who he was talking about, but did not allow anyone to be picked out by the general reading public. The Spanish nobleman's guests included Colonel A; Major B and his two daughters Miss B and the other Miss B; Mr and Mrs H with their daughter Miss H; Mrs G and finally 'the old Spanish nurse'.

After setting the scene and describing the arrangements in the house, Sanders said that one night there was 'a tremendous thumping on the doors, heavy footsteps along the passages and similar disturbances heard by every inmate of the house, including the servants'. He went on in some detail:

*The same thing happened with variations almost nightly for the succeeding two months that I was there, and every visitor that came to the house was disturbed in the same manner. One gentleman (Colonel A) told me he was awakened on several occasions with the feeling that someone was pulling the bedclothes off him. Some heavy footsteps were heard, and others like the rustling of a lady's dress; and sometimes groans were heard, but nearly always accompanied with heavy knocking: sometimes the whole house would be aroused. One night I remember five gentlemen meeting at the top of the stairs in their night suits, some with sticks or pokers, one had a revolver, vowing vengeance on the disturbers of their sleep.*

*During the two months after I first heard the noises I kept watch altogether about twelve times in various parts of the house, mostly unknown to others (at the time), and have heard the noises in the wing as well as other parts.*

*When watching I always experienced a peculiar sensation a few minutes before hearing any noise. I can only describe it as like suddenly entering an ice house, and a feeling that someone was present and about to speak to me. On three different nights I was awakened by my bedclothes being pulled off my feet. But the worst night I had at Ballechin was one night about the second week in September, and I shall never forget it as long as I live.*

*I had been keeping watch with two gentlemen, one a visitor the other one of the house. We heard the noises I have described about half past two. Both gentlemen were very much alarmed; but we searched everywhere, but could not find any trace of the ghost or cause of the noises, although they came this time from an unoccupied room. (I may mention that the noises were never heard in the daytime but always between midnight and four in the morning – generally between two and four o'clock.) After a thorough search the two gentlemen went to bed sadder, but not wiser, men, for we had discovered nothing. I then went to my room, but not to bed, for I was not satisfied, and decided to continue the watch alone. So I seated myself on the service stairs.*

*I had not long to wait (about twenty minutes only) when the knocking re-commenced from the same direction as before, but much louder than before and followed, after a very short interval, by two distinct groans which certainly made me feel very uncomfortable for it sounded like someone being stabbed and then falling to the floor. That was enough for me. I went and asked the two gentlemen who had just gone to bed if they had heard anything. One said he had heard five knocks and two groans, the same as I had; while the other (whose room was much nearer to where the sounds came from) said he had heard nothing. I then retired to my bed, but not to sleep, for I had not been in bed three minutes before I experienced the sensation as before, but instead of being followed by knocking, my bedclothes were lifted up and let fall again – first at the foot of my bed, but gradually coming towards my head. I held the bedclothes around my neck with my hands, but they were gently lifted in spite of my efforts to hold them. I then reached around me with my hand, but could feel nothing. This was immediately followed by my being fanned as though some bird was flying around my head, and I could distinctly hear and feel something breathing on me. I then tried to reach some matches that were on a chair by my bedside, but my hand was held back as if by some invisible power. Then the thing seemed to retire to the foot of my bed. Then I suddenly found the foot of my bed lifted up and carried around towards the window for about three or four feet, then replaced to its former position. All this did not take, I should think, more than two or three minutes, although at the time it seemed hours to me. Just then the clock struck four, and being tired out with my long night's watching, I fell asleep.*

No wonder the unfortunate man would never forget his experiences. Once the butler had gone into print, others involved also contacted *The Times* newspaper. Miss B wrote a letter a few days later in which she reported:

*I wakened suddenly in the middle of the night, and noticed how quiet the house was. Then I heard the clock strike two and a few minutes later there came a crashing, vibrating batter against the door of the outer room. My sister was sleeping very soundly, but she started up in a moment at the noise, wide awake. We heard the battering noise again two nights later when we were in the bedroom of our host's daughter waiting for the ghost.*

Major B then wrote in, having first taken the trouble to contact Colonel A, whose bedroom had been separated from his own by a wall with an interconnecting door.

He wrote:

*On August 24th at about 3.30am, I heard very loud knocking, apparently on the door to Colonel A's room, about nine raps in all. Three raps came quickly one after the other, then three more the same, and three more the same.*

*It was as if someone was hitting the door with his fist as hard as he could hit. I left my room at once, but could find nothing to account for the noise.*

*It was nearly daylight at the time. I heard the same noises on the 28th and 30th August at about the same hour viz. between 3 and 4am.*

*Butler Harold Sanders wrote a detailed account of his experiences at the hands of the poltergeist at Ballechin House*

Colonel A. corroborated the story, writing:

> *What I heard was what you heard, a terrific banging at one's bedroom door, generally about from 2 to 3am, about two nights out of three.*

Major B and the Colonel were on opposite sides of a partition door, yet both heard the same bangs and both thought they were coming from the other side. Mrs G also wrote to the newspaper.

> *I, my daughter, and my husband were put in rooms adjoining, at the end of the new wing. At 2am a succession of thundering knocks came from the end of our passage, re-echoing through the house, where it was heard by many others. About half an hour afterwards my husband heard a piercing shriek; then all was still. The next night and succeeding ones we heard loud single knocks at different doors along our passage. The last night but one before we left, I was roused from sleep by hearing the clock strike one, and immediately it had ceased six violent blows shook our own door on its hinges, and came with frightful rapidity, followed by deep groans.*

The most dramatic aspects of the visitation seem to have ended as soon as the Spanish family moved out. However, the correspondence in *The Times* intrigued a Miss Goodrich Freer, who proceeded to rent the house with the intention of investigating what she firmly believed to be a haunting by a ghost. Very soon after arriving, Miss Freer and her friends unpacked a ouija board and tried to contact the 'spirits' in a seance. They were rewarded by apparently being contacted by a spirit that called itself Ishbel, which instructed them to 'go at dusk to the glen up by the burn'. Miss Freer duly went to the specified place and waited. She recorded what happened next in a journal:

> *Against the snow I saw a slight, black figure, a woman, moving slowly up the glen. She stopped and turned and looked at me. She was dressed as a nun. Her face looked pale. I saw her hand in the folds of her habit. Then she moved on, as it seemed, on a slope too steep for walking. When she came under the trees she disappeared.*

Miss Freer appears to assume that the nun was Ishbel. However, did 'Ishbel' vanish in supernatural fashion or simply slip out of sight in the dark shadows that are to be found under fir trees at dusk? In the days that followed, Miss Freer and her guests reported hearing footsteps, bangs, knockings, crashes and groans in the house at night. Then Miss Freer, but nobody else, saw the ghostly nun three more times in the grounds of the house. On one occasion the ghost appeared to be weeping. Miss Freer undertook some research into the history of Ballechin House and found that about half a century earlier it had been home to a bad-tempered old man who had habitually threatened to 'come back and haunt' any local folk who annoyed him.

## The Haunting at Bethony

Another lady who took it upon herself to investigate a 'haunting' was a Miss Sharpe, who lived at Bethony, a manor house near Tackley in

Oxfordshire. In 1875 a former owner, Mr Bartholomew Chaundry, died after he fell over the banisters from the first floor. He landed in the hall and broke his neck. There were no suspicious circumstances, because Chaundry was a notorious drunk who was well known for falling over when he had been drinking heavily. Nevertheless, Miss Sharpe thought that the death might have had something to do with later events.

Miss Sharpe lived alone, though various friends and relatives came to visit from time to time. She also took in the village poor when they were ill – at least three of them died in the house, though she does not seem to have thought this significant. The house also contained a number of servants, but in her account of the 'haunting' Miss Sharpe does not say how many, nor does she name them.

The first sign of something odd happening came on 24 April 1905 when the sound of a door being slammed shut was heard. Other doors were heard being slammed, even when no door was found to be shut. After a few days of this, an odd sound rather like that of heavy metal chains being dragged over the roof was heard at night. Then came the faint sounds of muttering voices. The actual words could not be made out, but the voices definitely seemed to be male.

One day there came the sound of an enormous explosion. The entire house shook to the blast. 'I thought it was an earthquake,' recorded Miss Sharpe. No other properties in the area had been affected and no sign of any explosion could be found. The blast seemed to herald the start of the real visitation. From that day onwards, Miss Sharpe, her servants and her guests were subjected to phenomena that became more frequent and more insistent. Day after day Miss Sharpe recorded a succession of sounds.

The noise of a man in heavy boots clumping up the staircase, then back down again, was particularly common.

A sound like a workman battering at stone with a pickaxe was often heard for hours on end. On other days it was as if a football were being kicked against the walls repeatedly. The sounds of tearing paper were occasionally heard, as was the noise of a woman in a heavy, rustling silk skirt walking about. On some days an incessant light tapping would sound out in the Blue Room, a sitting room. Indeed, as the months passed it became clear that most of the phenomena took place in or adjacent to the Blue Room.

Objects were moved about – clothing was a favourite of the 'ghosts' – and bedclothes were torn off sleeping guests in the middle of the night. Others had their beds shaken violently from side to side. Strange sights were also seen. Lights akin to small stars were sighted floating through the house at night, while bright flashes would illuminate rooms for a second or two, then fade. Conversely candles would sometimes 'misbehave'. Although they could be seen to be as alight as ever, the light from them could dim as dramatically as if a cover of smoked glass had been put over them.

Then the apparitions began to appear. The first one to appear was what looked like the shadow of a burly man. Miss Sharpe took this to be the man in heavy boots who tramped up and down the stairs. The shadow became firmer until it assumed the definite shape of a big man in farming clothes. After materializing several times in a bedroom the burly farmer was seen no more. He was replaced by the more sinister figure of a tall, thin man wrapped in a black cloak. This spirit exuded a feeling of derision and scorn that was felt by everyone who saw him. Miss Sharpe did not content herself with merely recording the events in her diary – she also carried out tests. Thin threads were strung across rooms where the apparitions walked but they were never found to be broken, even after one of the figures had walked right through them. She sealed up rooms where noises were heard in order to make sure that nobody could get in or out, but the noises continued.

After some nocturnal disturbances upset a young niece who was visiting, Miss Sharpe decided that the intrusions had to stop, so she called in the local vicar.

On 12 July 1907 he conducted a prayer meeting in the house and sprinkled holy water in every room. According to Miss Sharpe the atmosphere in the house changed suddenly and definitively, and the manifestations ceased at once. In January 1908 strange noises began to be heard again. The most frequent sound this time was that of an invisible dog running about, its claws scritch-scratching on the wooden floors. Miss Sharpe sent for the vicar again and the service was repeated on 21 February. The manifestations ceased again, this time for good.

## The Case of 50 Berkeley Square

The visitations that I have discussed so far were fairly well documented because somebody on the scene chose to write down what was happening. Most incidents from the middle and later 19th century are not so well recorded. A typical instance was the case of 50 Berkeley Square, in London's prestigious Mayfair area, which was said to be the most haunted house in London. By the 1870s numerous stories were circulating about the house, but most of them refer to some sort of nameless horror on the top floor and a room at the back of the house that was said to be the most haunted of all.

In one version of the story a pair of sailors had spotted that the house was empty, so they broke in. After making free with the food and drink, they went upstairs to sleep. Early the following morning a passing policeman found the body of one of the sailors impaled on the railings outside the house. He had clearly fallen from a broken window high above. The policeman then broke into the house to search it. He found the second sailor on the upstairs floor – he was a gibbering wreck. The sailor muttered something incoherent about the horror that he had seen, but he never recovered his wits and died soon afterwards.

Another tale has it that the house was left empty for many years by the owner, who refused to rent it out to anybody. He employed a housekeeper who was instructed to keep the house in good order, but she was absolutely banned from going up to the top floor. The haunted room was kept securely locked and only the house owner had a key. Once every few months the owner would visit the forbidden room. He would lock the housekeeper in the kitchen and then climb the stairs. After unlocking the door he would go into the room and sit there for several hours. Then he would carefully lock the door behind him again and let the housekeeper out of the kitchen.

It was rumoured that a man who knew the owner once asked for permission to enter the haunted room. Against his better judgement the owner handed over his keys and the man travelled to London. The

*One man met his death, so the story goes, when he fell from an upper floor at No. 50 Berkeley Square and impaled himself on the railings. The body was discovered by a patrolling policeman*

housekeeper prepared the man's supper and then retired to bed. In the middle of the night the bell connected to the pull in the haunted room gave a gentle tinkle that awoke the housekeeper. Thinking that the guest might want a snack or a new chamber pot, she slipped on a dressing gown. At that point the bell was almost yanked off the wall by the violence of the tugging on the wire. The housekeeper hurried up the stairs with a light. She found the man stone dead on the floor with a look of absolute terror on his face.

Although such stories were widely known, there is absolutely no documentary evidence for any of them. It is known that for much of the preceding 40 years the house had been occupied by a rather eccentric man who did little to maintain it. No doubt the house did look like a haunted house at times. However, the origin of the stories seems to have been a poltergeist visitation in the 1850s. Nothing was written about it at the time, but later on those involved recollected that furniture had been moved about by unseen hands and various thumps and knockings had been heard. It is not much of a record of a poltergeist visitation, but it is sadly typical of much of the material from the time.

## Poltergeists in the News

In the second half of the 19th century, the population of Britain became almost universally literate for the first time. Accordingly, a large number of newspapers and magazines flooded the market. While earlier journals had been written by the gentry for the gentry, these new publications were aimed at the masses. It took a huge amount of material, from the sentimental to the sensational, to satisfy the appetites of this new reading public. Reports of mysterious happenings were particularly popular. Looking back, it can be seen that a good number of these stories describe some sort of poltergeist activity. The lack of any form of serious investigation meant that the details were sketchy, but the articles are an indication that the poltergeist phenomenon was continuing throughout these decades.

In August 1856, for instance, the newspapers in Bedford covered an odd story – it came to light at a judicial hearing. Mrs Moulton's husband was away for a few days on business, so on 12 August she decided to take the opportunity to fumigate their house. Together with the housemaid, Anne Fennimore, Mrs Moulton obtained the required sulphur and borrowed the 'burning jars' made of earthenware that would be needed. The jars were filled with sulphur, distributed around the house and ignited. At first all went well and the fumes began to fill the house, but then one of the burning jars suddenly toppled over, scattering flaming sulphur over the floor. The two women put the blaze out without much difficulty, though the floorboards had been singed, and the rest of the process passed off without trouble. However, as the women were preparing for supper that evening Mrs Moulton smelled burning again. She tracked it down to a spare bedroom where a mattress was on fire. She put the fire out with a jug of water and then called for the maid. Neither of them could think how the mattress had caught fire when none of the burning pots had been in the room.

Then they both smelled burning again. This time the smoke trail led to a blanket chest in another bedroom. The lid was opened to reveal a smouldering blanket, which was quickly extinguished. Then smoke came pouring out of a wardrobe. Opening the door, they discovered that a dress was on fire. There were no more incidents that day, but on the following morning some bed linen burst into flames. That was enough for Mrs Moulton – she sent an urgent telegram to her husband, demanding that he cut short his business trip and come home at once. Over the next few days at least a dozen small fires broke out around the house. A neighbour came round to keep Mrs Moulton company, but when she picked up a cushion from the sofa to plump it up it burst into flames in her hands.

Mr Moulton returned on 16 August. It was raining heavily so his overcoat got very wet as he walked back from the railway station. He hung the sodden garment up as he came in. A few hours later it was still just as wet, but it caught fire and the flames had to be beaten out. Mr Moulton sent for the police. While the policeman was talking to Mr Moulton, the handkerchief in his pocket suddenly burst into flames. Not knowing what to do, the policeman left after suggesting a judicial hearing. By the time the hearing took place in late August the fires had stopped occurring.

Witnesses were called to testify to the reality of the fires, but none of them were able to say what had started them. Mrs Moulton suggested that the spilled sulphur had somehow been to blame, but nobody could imagine quite how. The jury recorded a verdict of accidental damage.

Then in 1878 the *Glasgow News* reported the arrest of a 12-year-old girl named Ann Kidner. A hayrick in her home village had been set on fire and the local policeman had come along to investigate. His suspicions were aroused by Ann's behaviour. Sobbing uncontrollably, she kept on saying that she had not touched the hayrick. The policeman immediately frogmarched her off to the farmhouse of John Shattock, who owned the hayrick. Young Ann worked there as a scullery maid.

When Shattock heard the news of the fire, he was upset but strangely unsurprised.

He was also unwilling to blame the girl. As the policeman sat down at the kitchen table to discuss the matter, a loaf of bread rose into the air, drifted across the room and came to rest on a sideboard. The policeman's reaction was to arrest Ann and haul her off to prison. However, the magistrate ordered her release a few days later.

In December 1904 and January 1905 the *Louth News* kept up a running commentary on a series of bizarre events at Binbrook Farm near Great Grimsby. The case began as one of suspected vandalism after some chickens had been found dead in the chicken house one morning. As the newspaper reported, the birds had been killed in an outlandish manner:

> *They have all been killed in the same weird way. The skin around the neck, from the head to the breast, has been pulled off, and the windpipe drawn from its place and snapped.*

After this had happened a couple of times, the farmer, Mr White, set a watch on his chicken houses – which between them held over 250 birds. This made no difference because the chicken killings continued even though no person or animal was ever seen approaching the chicken houses. Then it seemed that the farmhouse had been broken into during the day. Furniture was found tumbled about, clothes had been hauled out of drawers and tossed about and ornaments had been moved from their usual places. The mystery deepened when the farmer and his family realized that nothing had been stolen. This happened at least a dozen times.

On 25 January the family gained a witness to the bizarre events when the village schoolteacher called. As he sat talking to Mrs White, the smell of burning wool drifted into the room.

They hurried out into the passageway and found a blazing blanket on the tiled floor. The blanket had not been there when the teacher had entered the house a few minutes earlier and there was no fireplace in the passage that could have set it on fire. Nor was there anyone else in the house. The teacher was sure of that. The climax to the visitation came three days later on 28 January. A reporter from the *Louth News* took down farmer White's account of the incident:

> *Our servant girl, whom we had taken from the workhouse and who had neither kin nor friend in the world that she knows of, was sweeping the kitchen. There was a very small fire in the grate: there was a guard there, so that no one can come within two feet or more of the fire, and she was at the other end of the room, and had not been near the fire. I suddenly came into the kitchen, and there she was, sweeping away, while the back of her dress was afire. She looked around as I shouted, and, seeing the flames, rushed through the door. She tripped and I smothered the fire out with wet sacks. But she was terribly burned and she is at the Louth Hospital now in terrible pain.*

The reporter then went to Louth Hospital. He was not allowed to talk to the girl, but the doctor told him:

> *The girl was burnt extensively on the back and lies in a critical condition. She adheres to the belief that she was in the middle of the room when her clothes ignited.*

That was the end of the visitation. The girl recovered and went to work elsewhere. By this time only 24 chickens were left alive.

I have included the following item to illustrate the fact that reports of the poltergeist phenomenon were not confined to the shores of Britain at this time. In December 1891 an outbreak of unexplained fires filled the newspapers in Toronto, Canada. The affected household was that of Robert Dawson and his wife. Also living in the house was 14-year-old Jennie Bramwell. Jennie's parents had died some years previously and she had been living in an orphanage. As was usual in those days, she had been trained in the skills useful to a domestic servant. The Dawsons had taken Jennie in a few months earlier and they were very pleased with her work and her character. In fact, they were considering adopting the girl and had been in touch with the orphanage about how they should go about it.

Jennie then fell ill. She could not get out of bed for several days and she kept slipping into a trance-like sleep that had the local doctor baffled. But on 11 December she made a sudden recovery, so she got up and returned to her usual routine. All went well until the following day, when a change came over her. She was chatting to Mrs Dawson in the sitting room when her eyes suddenly glazed over. When Mrs Dawson realized that the girl was not listening to her she thought that Jennie's mystery ailment had returned. Then Jennie seemed to snap out of it. She looked at Mrs Dawson in bewilderment and then her eyes went towards the ceiling. 'Look at that,' exclaimed the girl. Mrs Dawson looked up and saw that flames coming from seemingly nowhere were licking at the ceiling. They managed to put the blaze out by throwing water at it. An hour later, Jennie drew Mrs Dawson's attention to another fire that had broken out spontaneously.

Mr Dawson did not at first believe the stories that he heard on his return. However, he soon changed his mind when the wallpaper beside him burst into flames as he sat talking to Jennie. Then a dress caught fire, followed by a sofa. In all 45 fires broke out in the following seven days. Jennie was in the room on each occasion, but she was nowhere near any of the outbreaks when they occurred. Then Jennie announced that she wanted to go back to the orphanage, so she packed her bags and left. No more fires broke out in the Dawson household and none occurred at the orphanage.

## The New Breed of Researchers

The visitations that were recorded in the second half of the 19th century gradually convinced researchers that some types of haunting could not be classed as ghosts. Ghosts could be seen but they were not heard and they could not move things around. Yet there were records of spirits that moved objects and made noises. However, at this time most researchers were more interested in spiritualists and mediums, or in those humans who claimed extraordinary powers such as the ability to levitate or to see into the future. But fascinating as these paranormal abilities might be, they do not represent poltergeist activity.

By the 1890s a few researchers were willing to go into haunted houses in order to view events for themselves. The term 'poltergeist' was not yet in widespread use, but these researchers looked back over recent cases of physical ghosts and began to draw some conclusions. As before, it was clear that poltergeists inhabited the places where people lived – they did not favour open spaces. Poltergeist manifestations had also changed little since the earlier reports – there were still knocking noises, bangs, thumps and moving objects. The only apparently new phenomenon was the lighting of fires. The Amherst poltergeist used matches, then a new invention, but in other visitations fires were started without matches.

It was also increasingly apparent that most of the 19th-century poltergeists selected a focus person. This feature can also be discerned in earlier cases, but the records from the 19th century tend to be more detailed. The people who were present in the house are listed as well as the phenomena that took place. Where this focus could be clearly identified it was usually found to be a young person, usually a girl, who was undergoing some sort of stress. Esther Cox had undergone an attempted rape just before the Amherst visitation began, while Jennie Bramwell had heard that she might be adopted. Other apparent focus persons may or may not have been in a similar position. Ann Kidner, for instance, was working as a servant on a farm some way from home. She might have been very unhappy, or she might have been quite content –

the records do not offer any clues. But at least we know that she was not living happily at home with her family.

And as before there is the possibility of trickery. Miss Freer's experiences at Ballechin House seem just a little too convenient. Seeing a ghostly nun in a glen after being instructed by a ouija board message to go there is very odd. Even more so when the 'ghost' appeared at dusk, close to where there were some shadowy trees into which it could 'vanish'. Perhaps her friends were having some fun with her. But as the new breed of researchers went out into the world to search for physical ghosts, they were armed with rather more knowledge than the well-meaning vicars and curious gentlemen who had gone before them. They still did not know what was causing the events, but they were prepared to be open-minded. Their research would add massively to the available knowledge.

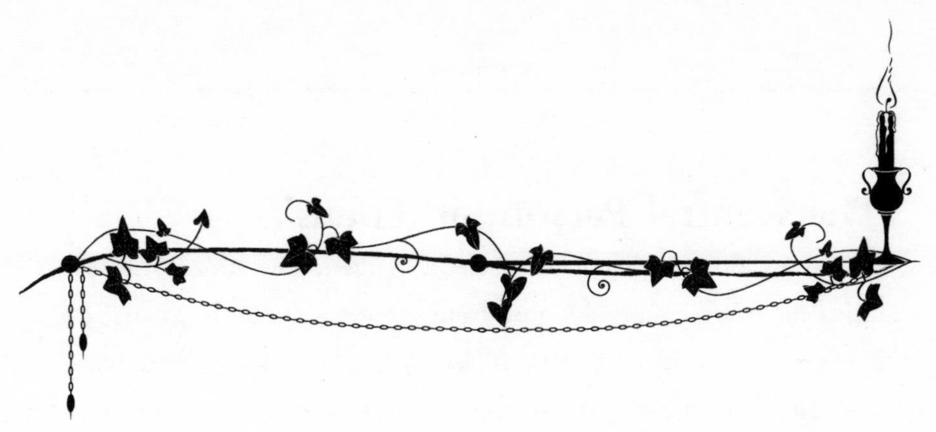

# chapter 5

# ENTER THE INVESTIGATORS

In the later 19th century specific organizations were created for the purpose of investigating anomalous phenomena. In Britain, these included the Ghost Club and the Society for Psychical Research (which quickly spread to the United States, Australia and continental Europe).

They were concerned with the idea that the soul survived physical death, but they also launched investigations into other odd phenomena – including poltergeists – and amassed a large amount of data.

# The Central Person, or 'Focus'

By about 1900 it was being recognized that physical hauntings, as many called them, were quite different from other hauntings. In particular, it began to be noticed that there was usually a central person, who was called the 'focus'. One of the earliest scientific researchers was the great criminologist Professor Cesare Lombroso of Italy. He kept copious notes and produced many theories about the possible cause of events.

Throughout the 1890s his studies of anomalous events encroached more and more on his official work. He soon became better known for his paranormal investigations, which were reported in the press, than for anything else. In November of 1900 Lombroso was in Turin when he read about a haunting in the local newspaper. It had taken place in a wine bar and restaurant in the Via Bava, whose proprietor was a Signor Fumero. This seemed to be a classic poltergeist visitation because the reports included accounts of furniture moving about, wine bottles smashing and ornaments dancing by themselves. Lombroso decided to investigate, so he went round to see Signor Fumero.

The investigation got off to a somewhat comical start when Lombroso knocked on the wine bar door one morning. He began by asking Fumero if the newspaper reports were accurate. Fumero replied, 'Oh yes, we did have a ghost. But it has gone away now. The famous Professor Lombroso came here a few days ago. He sorted the business out. There is nothing to see here.' Lombroso was most surprised to hear that he had supposedly already called, so he introduced himself and handed over his card. Fumero glanced hurriedly around the street, then ushered Lombroso inside. It

*Professor Cesare Lombroso was a criminologist who began to study the paranormal in the 1890s and produced a number of influential theories about the events he investigated*

turned out that the police had been called in a few days earlier. They had witnessed the bizarre events for themselves, but had assumed that Fumero was faking the visitation. They told him to stop the charade at once or they would arrest him for criminal damage, fraud and other unspecified crimes. Unnerved by this reaction, Fumero had decided to avoid any additional problems by claiming that Lombroso had visited his premises and solved the haunting. Now that Lombroso really was in his shop, he begged the famous professor to investigate.

Fumero ushered Lombroso down to his wine cellar. As the two men entered, a bottle flew across the room and struck Lombroso on the foot. Then three empty bottles rolled across the floor at great speed, smashing themselves to pieces against a table leg. The glass splinters joined a sizeable pile of other debris. Lombroso took a candle and began to walk around the cellar. He wanted to make sure that nobody was hiding there. His progress was halted when a bottle floated off a rack and drifted slowly through the air, before suddenly smashing itself on the floor. A second bottle repeated the manoeuvre, then a third, a fourth and a fifth. Lombroso decided to retreat upstairs with Fumero to discuss events. As they left another bottle smashed itself.

Once upstairs, Fumero explained that while most of the phenomena occurred in the cellar, strange events had taken place throughout the shop. Chairs had danced about in the front room, plates had floated around the kitchen and ornaments were always being found in the wrong places. Finally Fumero showed Lombroso a machine that had been thrown across the workroom by unseen hands. The main metal plate was badly bent. Lombroso decided that such a feat could not be achieved with a person's bare hands – indeed, a burly blacksmith armed with the tools of his trade would have had trouble replicating the damage.

Fumero told Lombroso that he had noticed one curious feature in the weeks since the disturbances began. Although the 'ghost' was in the habit of hurling bottles, knives and plates at people, the objects always missed by the narrowest of margins. For instance, a bottle of wine had recently been thrown at him with some force. But while it had been so close to his head that his hair had been splattered with wine when it had smashed itself against a wall, he had not been hurt. Nor had anyone else. It was as if the ghost wanted to frighten people but not actually hurt them.

Lombroso set about his investigation with methodical patience. He interviewed everyone involved and made a list of all of the incidents. Having studied all of the data, he came to the conclusion that the focus in this case was Fumero's wife, a nervous and skinny woman who was aged about 50. He suggested that Signora Fumero might like to take a short holiday as an escape from the stress of the haunting. The woman agreed with eagerness and made arrangements to stay with a cousin.

The 'haunting' stopped as soon as Signora Fumero left. When she came back, the manifestations began again. She reported that while she had been away she had suffered a recurrence of a strange illness that she had suffered as a teenager – she saw people who were not really there. Lombroso was convinced that he had found the focus but he wanted to double-check his theory, so he asked Signora Fumero to go away for a second time. However, the woman was reluctant to go in case this triggered her hallucinations. She believed that she was being driven from her home by the 'ghost', so before she left she launched into a long and bitter tirade against whatever it was.

This time the manifestations did not cease once the woman had left, but they changed dramatically. The disturbances now centred around the main bar and the kitchen areas. Not only that, they seemed to be confined to the pieces of kitchen equipment that had been used most often by the absent Signora Fumero. The objects used by the staff remained unaffected. When Signora Fumero returned the new pattern of disturbances continued. If she laid a table, the plates and the cutlery would immediately fly off towards the floor. If one of the staff laid a table nothing happened to it. Lombroso went back to his notes and studied them again. It was true that the problems appeared to revolve around Signora Fumero, but there was another factor. The disturbances only seemed to take place when a particular member of staff was on duty – a boy of about 14 who was thin, pale and rather introspective. When Lombroso asked Fumero to give the boy a day off the disturbances ceased. The trial was repeated, and again all was quiet. Fumero sacked the boy and the haunting came to a halt.

Lombroso accepted the conventional view that a poltergeist visitation is caused by a ghost, or the spirit of a dead person. He also believed that focuses were mediums who were not conscious of their ability to communicate with the dead. In the case of the Turin wine shop, he suspected that either the young waiter or a spirit that acted through him had a grudge against Signora Fumero. This would have explained why she was the target of the visitation while the actual focus was the young waiter. Lombroso died nine years after this investigation, having done much to popularize his theory that poltergeist activity occurred when an

*While Lombroso was in the Turin wine cellar, bottles of wine floated off the racks by themselves, hovered in mid-air and then smashed themselves on the floor*

angry or mischievous spirit managed to 'break through' into our world using an unconscious medium, the focus.

## Ghost in a Blacksmith's Shop

In Austria, the local branch of the Society for Psychical Research was presented with a poltergeist case in the summer of 1906. Herr Warndorfer was sent to investigate. On his arrival, he found a small blacksmith's workshop run by a Herr Zimmerl, who was assisted by two teenage apprentices. Zimmerl's problems began in July, when tools and pieces of metal were found to have been moved. Things escalated pretty rapidly, to the point that objects moved about when the men were in the workshop. By the end of July tools and iron bars were being flung about violently, though nobody was hit or injured.

Nevertheless, the manifestations were causing a nuisance. More than one customer narrowly avoided being struck by a flying lump of iron and the apprentices refused to work alone. Herr Zimmerl sent for the police, who at first assumed that one of the apprentices was causing the mischief. However, after they had seen some of the flying objects for themselves they pronounced themselves baffled, so they left. Which was when Herr Warndorfer arrived. He spent several days at the workshop, during which time he too witnessed the flying missiles. Although he was struck three times by tools or pieces of iron he felt only the lightest of touches and was quite uninjured. One day Herr Warndorfer had his pipe wrenched from his mouth by unseen hands. It hovered in front of his face for a second or two before flying off across the room. Warndorfer was intent on spotting any trickery so he kept a careful eye on Zimmerl and his apprentices. He found no evidence of any fraud or fakery, though the mayhem continued unabated.

In Britain, the cause of poltergeist research was taken up and advanced by the controversial Harry Price. Nobody has ever equalled Harry Price's stature as a ghost hunter. His carefully researched books contain a vast wealth of information and his lengthy investigations used the very latest technological gadgets. He was adept at finding natural explanations for alleged hauntings and he did not hesitate to speak out when he suspected trickery or fraud. At the same time, he would happily declare a phenomenon to be genuine if he thought that was the case. He billed himself as the greatest ghost hunter alive and he was accepted as such by the public and the media.

His fellow researchers into psychic phenomena were not so sure. In the latter part of his career Price was accused of fraud and trickery on several occasions. But while many suspected him of faking some of the phenomena he was supposedly investigating, nothing was ever conclusively proved. It is certain that he hammed up or exaggerated some of his claims in order to get the newspapers and the radio interested in his work or to boost sales of his books.

But that is quite a different thing from saying that he faked psychic phenomena. It is possible that some of the more diligent and retiring researchers resented Price's colourful showmanship. Perhaps they alleged trickery when all he was guilty of was announcing results without having conducted the tests that others thought were necessary.

Price was born in London in 1881. Little is known about his parents. He received a good, but unspectacular education at the Haberdashers' Aske's

*Ghost hunter extraordinaire Harry Price, who dealt with numerous poltergeist cases during his long and often controversial career*

Hatcham Boys School. During his time at school he read voraciously and his interest ranged over a vast array of subjects. He first displayed a liking for being in the public eye when he was a teenager. For instance, he enjoyed amateur dramatics and he wrote articles for the local press on various historical subjects. He also took an interest in the archaeological excavations in Greenwich Park, London, though how deeply he was actually involved is unclear.

After leaving school he worked as a paper salesman, but he continued to write for the newspapers. He also carried on playing an amateur role in archaeological digs. When he got married he dropped archaeology in order to become an amateur conjurer. He joined the Magic Circle in 1922. Inspired by Harry Houdini's unmasking of false mediums, Price also began using his conjuring skills to expose fraudsters. Like Houdini, his targets were the heartless people who were claiming to be able to communicate with the spirits of deceased loved ones. In order to further these investigations, Price established what he called the National Laboratory of Psychical Research, with himself as chairman.

In 1934 the National Laboratory was to become the University of London Council for Psychical Investigation, with Price as honorary secretary. Price continued his researches, radio broadcasts, writing and stage shows up to his death in 1948.

## The Battersea Mystery House

On 19 January 1929 Price paid his first visit to the Battersea Mystery House that is featured in the introduction to this book. He found the

Robinson family at breakfast. The house was home to 86-year-old Henry Robinson and his four adult children: Frederick, Lillah, Kate and Mary. Mary had been married to George Perkins, who had died a few months earlier. She had recently moved into the house with her 14-year-old son Peter. Frederick Robinson was the effective head of the household because the elderly Henry was mostly confined to his bed.

When Price called, Frederick began by showing him the broken glass in the conservatory and a couple of smashed ornaments. He then explained that he and his sisters were about to leave for work, while young Peter had to go to school. Price asked if he could come back after work along with a reporter from the *London Evening News*: Frederick agreed. When Price and the reporter, a Mr Grice, arrived late that afternoon, Frederick told them what had been happening. Price instantly realized that a poltergeist was at work.

After the dramatic opening barrages of coal and coins, the poltergeist had started creating fires. The Robinsons had a washerwoman who came in to launder the family's clothes and household linen. When she had unlocked the outhouse on 19 December she had been confronted by a heap of burning coals in the middle of the floor. She ran to fetch Frederick, who could not imagine how they had got there. Frederick and the washerwoman were the only two people with a key to the building, and neither of them had set the fire. Three days later an hour of mayhem began at 9am, when a loud banging noise was heard coming from the walls of the house. It was as if somebody was pounding on them with sledgehammers. Then the window in old Mr Robinson's bedroom exploded as if a large stone had been thrown through it. No stone was found, but the shards of glass were scattered all over the floor. The elderly man was understandably in a state of abject terror. Frederick ran out to ask a neighbour, Mr Bradbury, if the old man could stay at their house for a day or two. Bradbury agreed and he came round to help Frederick move the old man. As they were lifting old Mr Robinson from the bed a heavy chest of drawers began swaying from side to side and then crashed face down on to the floor.

As soon as the old man had left the house the hatstand in the hallway began rocking from side to side. Frederick ran to grab it, but it was wrenched from his hands by some invisible force. It was then flung against the stairs so violently that it broke in two. Bradbury came back at this point. He later told Price what had happened:

> *One of the women [Lillah] said that she was afraid to stop in the house, and that she was also afraid to go into her room to pack up her clothing. We went with her into her room, and she told us that she had been awakened by loud bangings on the door, and the crashing of glass. We stayed there until she had packed her bag and then returned to the back bedroom. Mr Robinson showed us pennies and coal on the conservatory roof.*
>
> *The four of us – all men – were looking at these when suddenly from another bedroom came a great crash and downstairs we heard a woman scream. We ran to the room and there we saw a chest of drawers lying on the floor. It was all very strange. Mr Robinson then took us to the kitchen and showed us the damage done there.*

Over the following two weeks the damage caused by the poltergeist had been less intensive, but the house was steadily becoming a shattered wreck. Panels had been smashed in three interior doors and nearly every window at the back of the house had been destroyed. Two more windows were damaged at the front. A tea tray and several plates and cups had been smashed and several ornaments had been thrown about and broken. Frederick Robinson showed Price and Grice around the house. He explained the damage and how it had occurred. When they walked into the house they stood for a moment in the scullery. As they did so there was a thump from the kitchen. They hurried through and found a wooden-handled gas lighter lying in the middle of the floor. It was normally kept on the gas stove. The reporter raced off to file a report just in time to make the stop press of his newspaper's evening edition.

Next day Price and Grice met to review and discuss the evidence. In the meantime, Grice had been doing some research. He had discovered that the house that backed on to Robinson's home was no normal house. It was, in fact, a private care home that was run by a psychologist who specialized in the care of men suffering from what was then called 'shell shock'. This term covered a range of mental disorders such as post-traumatic stress, nervous breakdown and intermittent insanity. The link between the various disorders was that they had all been brought on by the First World War.

At first it had been thought that shell shock was caused by the physical concussion of constant artillery fire. But by 1917 it began to be recognized that the problem was linked to the intensive strain of being in a war situation. It was also seen that more than one condition was involved. The term shell shock was dropped by doctors and the military, but it continued in common usage.

Although the First World War had been over for more than ten years by the time Price called at the Battersea Mystery House, hundreds of men were still so incapacitated by shell shock that they were unable to work. The poorer families cared for such men at home, but those with more money might place their relatives in private institutions such as the one in Battersea. It was well known that men suffering from shell shock were capable of erratic and often bizarre behaviour. Were the happenings at the Battersea Mystery House somehow related? Grice suggested that the missiles that had been falling on the Robinson household could have been thrown by the patients at the home. The distance from one house to the next was only 80 yards (73 metres), which was well within range of a catapult – the rear garden of the clinic was even closer. Price was not convinced by this theory, and neither was Grice, but they agreed to alert the doctor to what was going on. The doctor proceeded to keep an eye on his patients, but nothing untoward ever took place.

In any case, when Price and Grice returned to the Robinson household it was clear that events had moved on considerably. On 20 December the police had arrested Frederick Robinson. He had been taken to a secure hospital where a psychologist was examining him as to his mental state. Apparently the police had suspected him of plaguing his own family and faking the events. A policeman was put on duty outside the house to guard against sightseers. However, the removal of Frederick had not affected the visitation – the loud thumps and bangs continued as before, accompanied by flying objects. On the Saturday evening the manifestations had stepped up to a new level of activity.

It all started when Mrs Perkins went into the dining room to lay

*March of the furniture: a terrified Mrs Perkins was chased out of the dining room and along the corridor by a procession of chairs*

the table for dinner. As she did so one of the dining chairs slid back from under the table as if pulled by invisible hands. It turned to face Mrs Perkins and then began to advance towards her. A second chair then repeated the movement, forming up behind the first. A third followed, then a fourth and a fifth. Understandably, Mrs Perkins quickly retreated into the hallway. But she was pursued by the chairs, which advanced in single file like soldiers on parade. The bizarre procession followed Mrs Perkins to the foot of the stairs and then the chairs turned around and marched back into the dining room. When Mrs Perkins summoned up the courage to go back into the room she found all of the chairs piled up on top of the dining table. After some minutes, during which nothing else happened, Mrs Perkins lifted the chairs down and began laying the table. She then went through to the kitchen to fetch some plates. When she returned the chairs were all stacked up on top of the table again. She took them down, but again they arranged themselves on top of the table. At that stage she was totally unnerved, so she went out to get the policeman who was on guard. He came in, looked at the chairs and accused Mrs Perkins of putting them there herself. She scolded him and sent him outside again.

Next day it was Kate Robinson's turn to witness a series of bizarre events. It began in mid-morning, when her brother's attaché case flew at her across the kitchen. She retreated to the hall, where an umbrella sprang from the hall stand and floated across the room. Later, when she was in the kitchen with Peter, the chairs started vibrating – then the kitchen table fell over. Kate and Peter ran outside and watched through the windows as the kitchen chairs jigged about and then all fell over at the same time.

There was much to tell Price and Grice when they visited the house on the following Monday. As they were talking to Kate and Mrs Perkins in the kitchen there came a loud thump from the scullery. Price and Grice hurriedly burst into the room to find a pair of lady's boots on the floor. Inside one of them was a bronze cherub. It was one of a pair of ornaments that were kept on the mantelpiece in the sitting room. The disturbances continued for the rest of the week, though not at the level that had been witnessed the previous weekend. On the following Friday Kate Robinson and Mrs Perkins decided to abandon the house. Young Peter was sent off to stay with relatives in the country on a long-term basis while the two women moved in with friends in Battersea.

That weekend the crowds gathered in Eland Road to gape at the Mystery House.

There were so many people squashed together that mounted police officers and several constables were in attendance. However, nothing was seen or heard. Price then got permission to spend some time alone in the house. On the following Monday, the *Daily Express* contacted him to see if he would allow a well-known medium to join his investigation. Price agreed, so when he went to the house on Wednesday of that week he was accompanied by the medium and a *Daily Express* reporter named Salusbury. Price does not seem to have had a high regard for the medium. In his review of the case written a few years later he says that the medium declared that she felt excessively cold when she entered the house. As Price points out, it was the middle of winter and the house had been locked up for several days without a fire being lit.

The party toured the house, going from room to room. The medium sensed nothing apart from the cold, which she thought was supernatural. After visiting all of the upstairs rooms the trio went back downstairs. They all noticed that a piece of yellow soap was now lying in the middle of the hall floor. All of them were certain that it had not been there earlier and none of them could explain how it got there. Mrs Perkins later identified it as a piece of soap from the washroom. Frederick Robinson was released by the police on the following day. He moved straight back into the house and Kate and Mrs Perkins followed a day or two later. When old Mr Robinson died a couple of weeks after their return the family finally abandoned the Mystery House and rented another one nearby. There were no further disturbances in Eland Road and the family had no problems in their new home.

Looking at the Battersea case with hindsight, it can be seen that the visitation followed the pattern that was by then becoming familiar to investigators. It began relatively quietly, with a few small pieces of coal being thrown. The disturbances then escalated, very quickly in this case, until they reached a dramatic crescendo – furniture started marching around the house. They ended abruptly when Peter Perkins was sent to live with relatives in the country. Apart from the appearance of a stray bar of soap nothing else happened after Peter left. This would seem to indicate that Peter was the focus of this particular poltergeist visitation. He certainly had some of the attributes of a focus. He was a teenager and his father had recently died, which had forced him and his mother to move into a rather crowded house with relatives. The situation cannot have been anything other than stressful. We also have no way of knowing how well or badly Peter got on with his relatives. The activities during this poltergeist visitation fit the general pattern. Objects were thrown about, furniture moved of its own accord and bangs and thumps were heard. Despite the mayhem, nobody was hurt.

## Gef the Mongoose

By the time of the Battersea Mystery House case many people were willing to accept the fact that unexplained events can sometimes take place. But when a poltergeist took the form of a talking mongoose it was generally accepted that the limits of credibility had been reached. The events took place at Doarlish Cashen on the Isle of Man during the 1930s and Price went along to investigate. However, because of the general mirth that the case had generated it was small wonder that he was rather cool about it in later years. Writing in 1945 he dismissed it as 'the talking mongoose case that I investigated, with negative results, in 1935'. Because he needed to earn a living from his investigations, Price did not relish being associated with a famous source of amusement, and so he probably preferred to keep his distance. However, a reappraisal of Price's notes, and those of other investigators, shows that the Doarlish Cashen visitation was a relatively straightforward poltergeist case, albeit with some very peculiar features.

In September 1931 the isolated farmhouse of Doarlish Cashen was home to the Irving family. There was James Irving, his wife Margaret and their 13-year-old daughter Voirrey. James was a retired salesman who had bought the smallholding to indulge his love of growing fruit and vegetables while creating an income to supplement his modest pension.

At 60 he was several years older than his wife. Voirrey was a quiet girl who did well at school but did not make friends easily. She was particularly keen on wildlife, having read a great deal about the subject. Living on the Isle of Man enabled her to study a wide range of wildlife at close hand.

The visitation began with the usual low-level activity. In this case it took the form of scurrying noises, accompanied by growling and barking as if some sort of animal was making a home for itself under the floorboards. Now and then there came a loud cracking noise that made the walls shake and the pictures move slightly. The Irvings decided that some sort of animal had taken up residence in their house, though the cracking phenomenon was a mystery. After several weeks of this, James Irving decided to see if the creature would respond to any of his animal impersonations – something for which he had quite a name in the area. He began with mammal noises, because the mystery animal seemed to be a mammal of some kind. The mysterious intruder accurately copied the calls of foxes, hedgehogs and badgers, but then it moved on to mimic local birds as well. In November the 'animal' began repeating rhymes sung by Voirrey, though in a very high-pitched and squeaky voice. There was no animal on earth that could do that.

By February 1932 the strange creature had learned how to talk in a more normal, human-like voice. It could also speak for itself – it did not just repeat what the Irvings said. Most of the talk was of a purely domestic nature.

The voice reminded Mrs Irving to do the ironing or suggested that Mr Irving should go to the shops. However, the intruder did sometimes talk about itself. It announced that its name was Gef and that it was a

*Doarlish Cashen: Voirrey Irving and her father stand outside the isolated farmhouse on the Isle of Man that was haunted by Gef the talking mongoose*

mongoose who had been born in Delhi on 7 June 1852. It stuck to this story throughout the visitation. The Irvings seem to have taken Gef's claims at face value. They believed that they were dealing with a talking mongoose of astonishing intelligence – they always spoke about the visitation in those terms. It was James Irving who brought the talking mongoose to Harry Price's attention. Price was busy on other projects, but he thought the case sounded interesting so he sent a friend, Captain MacDonald, to investigate.

MacDonald arrived at Doarlish Cashen on 26 February 1932. Although he stayed for more than five hours, and gathered much information from the Irvings, he experienced nothing odd. Eventually he got up to leave, saying that he would return on the following day. At once Gef's voice called out, 'Go away. Who is that man?' Then came a string of indistinct mutterings. When MacDonald returned, nothing much happened at first. Then a stream of water emerged from a wall – the Irvings told MacDonald it was Gef 'performing its natural functions'. A short while later Gef began talking to Margaret while she was upstairs. MacDonald, who was downstairs, called out to Gef, but the talking mongoose replied, 'No, I won't stay long as I don't like you.' MacDonald tried creeping up the stairs, but Gef heard him and called out, 'He's coming.' No more was heard of Gef that day.

A reporter from the *Daily Dispatch* in Manchester then paid a short visit. He heard the voice of Gef, but no other manifestations took place while he was there. When an old family friend named Charles Northwood went to visit the Irvings in March 1932, Gef became a little more voluble. The story of Gef the talking mongoose had appeared in the newspapers

and Northwood seems to have been concerned about his friends, so he arranged to visit for a few days. Before he arrived, he asked James Irving if he thought Gef would be active during his visit. Northwood was perhaps initially disappointed, because Gef was quiet when he first arrived. He did not speak or scurry about and he did not sing his favourite song, *Carolina Moon*, even when it was played on the gramophone. But when Voirrey went into the kitchen to prepare lunch she heard Gef whisper, 'Go away, Voirrey, go away.' After lunch Gef's voice became louder and Northwood heard him call out, 'Charles, Charles, Chuck, Chuck.' Gef then returned to his usual domestic chatter about farm affairs. When Northwood suggested that his son Arthur might like to visit, Gef reacted violently. 'Tell Arthur not to come,' Gef shouted. 'He doesn't believe. I won't speak if he does come. I'll blow his brains out with a thrupenny cartridge.' There followed a long period of silence. Then Gef shouted at Northwood, 'You don't believe. You are a doubter.' This outburst was followed by loud bangs and crashes. Then there was silence again until after Northwood had gone.

In the months that followed, Gef performed only when the Irvings were alone. He had apparently taken up residence in a wooden box in Voirrey's bedroom – it was here that he was heard most often. Gef also began to indulge in the more physical antics that were associated with poltergeists. He moved chairs around, he bounced a rubber ball in time to music on the gramophone, he opened drawers and rummaged about in them and he struck matches. More unusually, Gef began killing rabbits and leaving them for the Irvings to find. He would announce a kill from his wooden box, which Voirrey began calling 'Gef's Sanctum', and then he would tell the Irvings where he had left it. The dead rabbit was always

*Marking his territory? A stream of water that inexplicably spurted from the walls was explained by the Irving family as being Gef the mongoose urinating*

there and it made a welcome addition to the family larder. Gef also took to eating food that had been left out for him. He ordered what he wanted – it was usually bacon, sausages or chocolate – and said where it should be put. The food would be taken as soon as the Irvings were not looking.

Gef was generally friendly and chatty, though his temper changed at times. When asked who he was, he once said, 'I am a ghost in the form of a weasel,' but on another occasion he said, 'I am the Holy Ghost.' He was perhaps being more truthful when he said, 'You will never get to know what I am.' Sometimes he was amusing – he would say, 'I am the eighth wonder of the world,' for instance, or 'I can split the atom.' But he could also be mildly abusive when he called people names and told them to leave the house. The reporter from the *Daily Dispatch* returned so that he could carry out a detailed investigation. This time he was rather more sceptical. He noticed that Gef spoke only when Voirrey was in the same room. Although he did not actually put his opinion into words, it is clear that he suspected that Voirrey was responsible for the voice.

Gef preferred not to be seen, though all three members of the family caught glimpses of something that could have been Gef. However, he invited Margaret to put her hand through a hole in Voirrey's bedroom wall on a couple of occasions. On her first attempt she felt a little paw with three long fingers and a thumb. When she had another try she felt Gef's mouth complete with his small, sharp teeth. Voirrey once took a photo of Gef, but the print was indistinct. It just showed a blob, which might have been a mongoose, or a weasel – or anything else for that matter.

In March 1935 Gef left Voirrey a memento. It was a tuft of what he said was his hair. James Irving sent the scraps of fur to Price, who had been monitoring the case. Price then had them analysed by London Zoo. The results showed that the hair had probably come from a domestic dog with slightly curly hair and a fawn colour. He consulted MacDonald who confirmed that the Irvings had a pet dog named Mona, which had wavy hair of a brown colour. Price decided that it was time he investigated the goings-on at Doarlish Cashen for himself.

He took Richard Lambert, editor of *The Listener* magazine, along with him to the Isle of Man. Gef did not appear during their stay so neither Price nor Lambert came away with any first-hand testimony. The two men did, however, collect witness statements from everyone who had experienced the phenomenon. They also took plaster casts of footprints that had apparently been left by Gef. The casts were sent to the experts at London Zoo, who replied that the footprints could not be precisely identified, though they might belong to a weasel or a raccoon. The experts were more definite about the hair samples that had been taken from the Irvings' pet dog Mona. They were absolutely identical to the fur that had supposedly come from Gef.

This fact has often been used as evidence that the Gef visitation was a fraud from start to finish. However, it must be said that many poltergeists are habitual liars. If Gef had claimed that the dog's hair was his own his behaviour would have been typical of a poltergeist.

As well as being investigated by Price, Gef was also studied by Nandor Fodor of the International Institute for Psychical Research. Fodor did not believe that Gef was either a mongoose or a ghost. He had a theory that poltergeists were created by the focus person, perhaps unconsciously. So the manifestations were generated by a human mind that was undergoing subconscious turmoil. He became convinced that the Gef visitation fitted in with his theories, but few others shared his views.

The Irvings reported that by the autumn of 1935 Gef was not as active as he had been. Early in 1936, he seems to have vanished altogether. The Irvings later sold up and moved away. In 1946 the farmer who had bought the property, Leslie Graham, shot and killed a weasel-like creature on the property. He contacted the newspapers and said that he had 'killed Gef the talking mongoose'. The newspapers showed Voirrey a photo of the animal, but she said it was not Gef. She seemed very certain of the fact.

Gef's antics had come in for some serious and detailed investigation during the five years that they had lasted. It is therefore possible to look at the case and its background in a more detailed way than was possible in earlier visitations. Gef showed all the characteristics of a typical poltergeist, in spite of his claims to be a mongoose. That is, the visitation had begun with infrequently heard low noises, which had become louder and more numerous over a period of some weeks. Finally, the manifestations had become more dramatic. The voice had started as animal grunts and barks and had then become high-pitched. At first it was able only to repeat what was said to it, but eventually it was apparently able to speak for itself with intelligence.

As in other poltergeist cases, it seems that Gef became what the Irvings expected him to be. Right from the start, the Irving family had interpreted the noises as being those of an animal. Even when the intruder began to speak, they remained convinced that they were dealing with a clever animal.

*The International Institute for Psychical Research sent Nandor Fodor to investigate Gef, whom he recognized as a poltergeist*

So when Gef finally talked about himself it was to announce that he was indeed a clever animal. Another feature of the case that seems to link it to other poltergeist visitations is the way in which the manifestations continued for a while and then tailed off. Gef was around for about five years in all, but he never seems to have produced the hugely dramatic stunts that some poltergeists of shorter duration have managed to achieve. This inverse correlation between duration and intensity of activity seems to be a feature of the cases that have been subjected to study. The longer a visitation has lasted the less impressive the manifestations have been.

The Irving family's circumstances were carefully noted by several visitors. There were elements that would characterize other poltergeist visitations. James Irving was a boastful fellow who liked to spin yarns to his neighbours about his exploits as a salesman. He had married late and he dominated his family. The household had been run according to his whim, with little regard for the wishes of Margaret or Voirrey. Margaret tolerated James's bossiness. She was seemingly content as long as she was generally left alone. Young Voirrey also seems to have accepted a subordinate role at home. At the same time, she shone academically at school and indulged her passion for wildlife studies in the fields and woods around her home. However, the remote nature of her home and her father's attitude did not allow her to bring school friends home. This was perhaps why she did not have any really close companions of her own age. Voirrey was undoubtedly the focus of this visitation. Many people who have been the focus of a visitation were finding life frustrating or stressful. Perhaps that was true in the case of Voirrey.

Another feature that surrounded the Gef visitation was a vague suspicion of trickery and fraud. It is one that has been seen in several other cases.

The reporter from the *Daily Dispatch* suspected that Voirrey might be making the voice of Gef, but he was never able to catch her out. Price also suspected fraud in the later stages of the case. Another reporter, this time from the *Isle of Man Examiner*, thought that James Irving was to blame. The journalist noted that when on one occasion Gef had given a rather indistinct squeak, James had said, 'There, you heard him. He said, "They don't believe." You heard him. That was Gef.' Gef had certainly said no such thing so James was guilty of exaggeration. But this was at the time when Gef's visits were getting less frequent and impressive. Perhaps James wanted to ensure that the reporter did not go home disappointed.

## The Case of Olive Wilkins

Altogether more conventional was a later case from Price's files, yet in some ways it was unique. The events involved a Dr Wilkins of Sunderland and his family and they took place in 1942. It all perhaps began in 1940, though, when Dr Wilkins' daughter Olive fell in love with a flight lieutenant in the RAF. She was only 19 and he was a few years older. The airman proposed, but Dr Wilkins and his wife were reluctant to give permission for the marriage to go ahead. Not only was Olive quite young but there was also a war on and her prospective husband was on active service. There was every possibility that their daughter might become a very young widow. After some debate, none of it bad-tempered, the young couple finally got married in the autumn of 1941. They set up home in a rented flat in Sunderland, where Olive had a job as a secretary. If her new husband was on duty, Olive would often go to her parents' home for supper. Because the rented flat was small, she had left many belongings – such as books, a tennis racket, old toys and the like – in her old bedroom.

On 26 February 1942 Mrs Wilkins borrowed a kilt pin from her daughter's jewellery box, so that she could secure a wrap. Nothing in the bedroom was out of place. After spending the day in town, Mrs Wilkins returned home, took off her wrap and went to her daughter's former bedroom. She was going to replace the pin while she remembered. As she entered the room she stopped dumbfounded. The bedclothes had been carefully and neatly turned down, just as they would have been if the family had still had a maid. Mrs Wilkins was certain that she had not touched the bed and nobody had a key to the house except herself, Dr Wilkins and Olive – both of whom were at work.

Three days later Mrs Wilkins was in the kitchen preparing dinner when she heard the front door open. The familiar sound of her husband's footsteps approaching across the hallway was heard, accompanied by the click-clack of her daughter's heels. The kitchen door opened and in came Dr Wilkins alone.

'Where is Olive?' asked Mrs Wilkins.

'I don't know,' replied Dr Wilkins. 'Gone home I suppose.' She was not with him, nor had he heard her footsteps.

Four days later, Mrs Wilkins went into Olive's room to find that the bed had been disarranged just as if it had been slept in. Two days later one of Olive's books had been removed from the bookcase and then left open on the windowsill. It was just as if somebody had glanced at it before putting it down. A week later Mrs Wilkins again heard the front door open. This time only one set of footsteps could be heard coming across the hallway. There was no mistaking Olive's tread, though. She went up the stairs, along the landing and into her bedroom. Then she came out again and went into the bathroom. The toilet flushed and then there was silence. After a while Mrs Wilkins went up but there was no sign of her daughter. When Dr Wilkins got home he was sent hotfoot round to Olive's flat, where he found the young couple sitting down to supper. Olive said that she had not been round to her parents' house at all. A couple of weeks later, Olive really did come round after work. She brought the happy news that she was pregnant. One month later her husband was posted overseas.

Olive's pregnancy developed along perfectly normal lines as the weeks passed. But at the home of Dr and Mrs Wilkins the poltergeist-like activity increased in frequency and variety. The bedclothes in Olive's old bedroom came in for particular attention.

They were found rumpled as if they had been slept in, stripped from the bed and folded neatly or turned down ready for a person to get into. Not only that – the drawers in Olive's dressing table had often been found open. The clothes they contained had often been rearranged or placed on the bed. Underwear was a favourite target for this treatment, but skirts and blouses were also moved about. Again and again Mrs Wilkins heard the sounds of her daughter opening the front door and walking across the hallway. Sometimes it really was her, but most of the time it was not. If Mrs Wilkins went into the hall the footsteps would stop at once, but if she did not the sounds would move up the stairs to Olive's bedroom. By the time Olive entered the final month of her pregnancy something was happening every day. Sometimes it was twice a day.

Thus far the disturbances had been restricted to the upper part of the house. Then one day Mrs Wilkins came home from shopping to find that something strange had taken place in the dining room. A photograph of her daughter and son-in-law that had been kept on the mantelpiece had been moved to the table. Fearing that this sudden change marked some problem, Mrs Wilkins telephoned her daughter's place of work. She discovered that she had gone into labour and had been taken to hospital. The next day Olive gave birth to a healthy baby girl, who was named Enid. The manifestations ceased at once and they never returned.

This case is interesting for a number of reasons. The disturbances at the Wilkins' home were in some ways typical of a poltergeist. They began slowly and they built up to a climax. Objects were moved about and unexplained sounds were heard. The manifestations also centred on a young person whose life had been recently disturbed.

In other ways the case was unique. The disturbances were very obviously linked to Olive's old home and her former bedroom. They were also centred on things that she had used before she was married.

The stress that Olive had been placed under must have been considerable. She had recently married, she was pregnant and her husband had been sent away to a dangerous place. Interestingly, the disturbances began when Olive discovered that she was pregnant. At such an emotional time she must have been drawn back to the security and safety of her old home, her toys and her bedroom. It would seem to be the case, therefore, that this entirely understandable longing manifested itself in poltergeist-type incidents. However, it is possible that Mrs Wilkins was the focus and that it was her anxiety for her daughter that was the emotional impulse behind the manifestations.

The cases studied by these early investigators were useful in that they revealed that a number of features regularly occur in poltergeist visitations. But however dramatic these earlier cases were, they are as nothing compared to the cases that have occurred since. In more recent decades the recipients of a visitation have been more willing to report what has been happening, while researchers have conducted investigations with ever greater thoroughness.

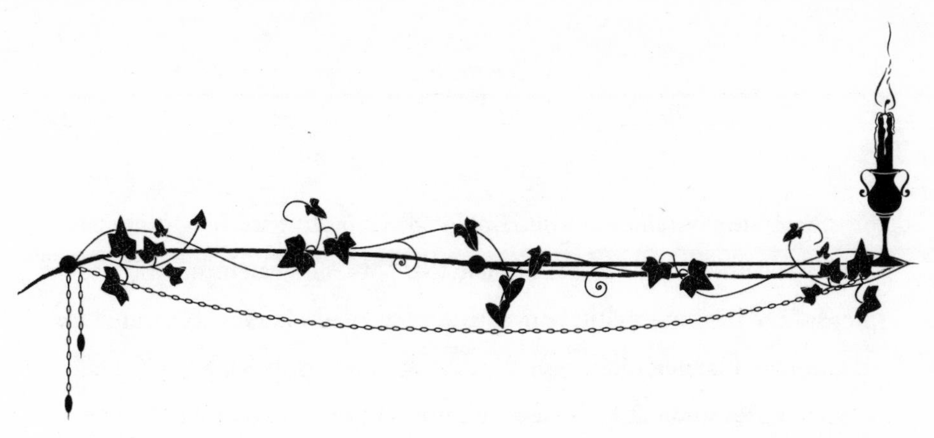

# chapter 6

# MAJOR INVESTIGATIONS

By the later 20th century the poltergeist phenomenon was beginning to be better recognized by the general public. That is not to say that it was better understood. Although the term 'poltergeist' was being widely used by lots of people, it was being loosely applied to a range of phenomena.

The result was that most people still tended to view a poltergeist as a form of ghost, not as a distinct type of paranormal event. Added to that,

most mainstream scientists continued to be reluctant to spend time and money investigating poltergeist visitations. Those few scientists who were prepared to deal with visitations seriously were not always able to get to the scene of a poltergeist visitation while it was still happening. Their frustration was shared by a large number of amateur investigators. As a result, phenomena were not always investigated as thoroughly as might have been hoped. Even so, these people were doing their best and a useful amount of evidence and data was compiled.

## The Sauchie Poltergeist

In the case of a poltergeist that occurred in the Scottish village of Sauchie in 1960 it was Dr A Owen, a fellow of Trinity College, Cambridge who launched an investigation. He visited the scene while the visitation was in progress and interviewed most of those concerned.

The focus of this poltergeist was apparently 11-year-old Virginia Campbell. She and her mother Annie had recently moved to Sauchie from Donegal in Ireland, following the divorce of Annie from Virginia's father. Virginia and Annie moved in with relatives, which meant that Virginia had to share a room with her nine-year-old cousin Margaret.

The move seemed to go well, though, and Virginia settled in comfortably at Sauchie School. Then on 22 November, just after Virginia and Margaret had gone to bed, something strange happened. The girls claimed to have heard the sound of a ball bouncing around in their room, but this ceased when Annie went up to investigate. Next day some furniture was found to have been moved.

*The house in Sauchie where Virginia Campbell lived during the poltergeist visitation*

That night the bouncing ball noises were back, but this time they were louder and more insistent. Over the following days the manifestations increased rapidly. Doors slammed shut or flew open by themselves; a heavy sideboard slid across the floor without anybody touching it. The disturbances only happened when Virginia was present. When the local vicar was called in he conducted a prayer service, but this produced no effect.

The poltergeist activity then began to go wherever Virginia went. Her schoolteacher, Miss Stewart, noticed this first. At the time she was unaware of the strange events at Virginia's home. One day the child sitting in front of Virginia got up to hand in some work. As she did so her desk rose about six inches into the air. The teacher thought she was seeing things, particularly when the desk drifted back to the ground after a few seconds. A couple of days later Miss Stewart saw Virginia behaving oddly. She was leaning on the lid of her desk, as if to stop it from opening.

Miss Stewart called out, which made Virginia look up. As she did so the desk lid opened slightly, as if something inside was trying to get out. Virginia hurriedly slammed it shut again.

Miss Stewart finally accepted that something very strange was going on when she called Virginia up to the front of the class. The teacher was sitting at her desk, a large heavy wooden affair that she could barely move without assistance. Virginia was standing to one side of Miss Stewart, with her hands folded behind her back. As Miss Stewart was talking she suddenly became aware that the children were no longer looking at her, but at her desk. She had rested the blackboard pointer on her desk when she had sat down and it was now rocking from side to side without anybody touching it. Then it stopped moving, only for the desk itself to start to shake. Slowly the desk began to rise into the air. Confused and alarmed, Miss Stewart put her hands on top of the desk and tried to push it back down to the ground, but without success. As soon as she let go the desk rose higher. Then it began to turn slowly. When it had moved through about 90 degrees it began to descend towards the floor. Miss Stewart then glanced at Virginia who was sobbing uncontrollably. Seeing the teacher's eyes on her, Virginia blurted out, 'I'm not doing it, Miss. Please, Miss. Honest I'm not.'

Miss Stewart first calmed Virginia down and then she dismissed the class. After talking to Virginia for a while she learned that similar things were happening at the girl's home. Virginia was adamant that she was not responsible for the events, though she knew that they only happened when she was around. Miss Stewart later summoned her class and explained to them very clearly that sometimes people got ill and that things might then happen that were not really their doing. One child asked if a ghost had been moving the desk. Miss Stewart very firmly put that idea down. She said that there was no ghost and that she would not stay in a room if she thought it was haunted. 'So long as I stay here, you are all right,' she concluded.

Strange things continued to happen at Virginia's school. A bowl of flowers moved across Miss Stewart's desk, for instance. But nothing was ever as dramatic as the moving desk. From then onwards most of the manifestations took place at Virginia's home. Ornaments were moved about – sometimes they floated through the air – and bedclothes were torn off in the middle of the night. Both Margaret and Virginia also felt themselves pinched awake by unseen hands. Annie noticed that the events followed a definite cycle. They built up to a crescendo for a few days and then they faded away. Dr Owen asked Annie to keep a diary of events, which proved that she was right. The cycle was one of 28 days. After about six months the strange phenomena began to tail off and finally they ceased entirely.

## The Black Monk of Pontefract

Although the events in Sauchie had been recorded by a responsible researcher while they were in progress, such was not the case during the visitation that became known as the Black Monk of Pontefract. In spite of the name given to the haunting, the link to any monk living or dead was tenuous. Perhaps a poltergeist was manifesting itself in the form of a monk in order to satisfy the expectations of those it was disturbing.

The visitation took place at 30 East Drive, a street on a fairly modern estate just outside the historic heart of Pontefract in Yorkshire. Living in the house when the disturbances began in August 1966 were Joe Pritchard, his wife Jean and their two children. Phillip their son was 15 years old and their daughter Diane was 12. Joe ran the town's pet shop and was considered to be a steady and reliable sort of a chap. Joe's brother and his wife Enid lived next door and Jean's sister Marie and her husband Victor lived a few doors away. Jean's mother, Mrs Sarah Scholes, lived further away but she was a frequent visitor and she sometimes came to stay.

The housing estate of which East Drive was a part had been built on a hill which had been open farmland when the building work had begun.

Until the 18th century a gallows had stood on top of the hill. It would have been some distance away from what is now East Drive. A stream had once run down the hillside. For those needing to cross the stream there had been a footbridge called Priest's Bridge. This bridge stood close to the future site of East Drive. However, when the estate had been built the bridge had been demolished and the drainage system on the hill had been changed.

The stream had then disappeared. None of this was known to the Pritchards in 1966, but they would discover it later and it would become significant.

In August 1966 Jean, Joe and Diane Pritchard went away on a family holiday to the West Country. Phillip wanted to stay at home, so Mrs Scholes agreed to stay with him at East Drive. The visitation began in spectacular fashion on a sunny but none too warm Thursday morning. Phillip was in the garden reading a book and Mrs Scholes was sitting in the living room knitting. Then at about 11.30am a gust of wind rattled through the house. Soon afterwards Phillip walked into the kitchen and put the kettle on. Then he went through to the living room to ask his grandmother if she wanted a cup of tea. What he saw made him stop in alarm and surprise. The entire room was filled with a cloud of fine white dust, rather like chalk dust. It was drifting slowly downwards to settle over the carpet and the furniture. Mrs Scholes spotted the dust at almost the same moment. She looked up and asked Phillip what he was up to. 'Nothing,' replied Phillip. 'What is this stuff?'

When Mrs Scholes stood up they both noticed that the dust did not actually fill the room but only the lower part of it – so the top half of their bodies rose above the dust cloud. The dust was falling, yet it seemed to be replenishing itself somehow.

A puzzled Mrs Scholes walked over to the house of her daughter, Marie Kelly, and asked her to come over. When Mrs Kelly ran round to East Drive she saw that everything in the living room was covered in a thin layer of white dust, although the dust had stopped falling. She was as puzzled as the others, but she had a practical bent and so she decided that whatever the dust was it needed cleaning up. Mrs Kelly went through to the kitchen to get a duster, pan and brush, but as she did so she almost slipped on a pool of water on the floor. Quickly grabbing a cloth, she mopped it up. But then she spotted a second pool of water and a third. She lifted the linoleum to search for the source of the water, but the concrete floor underneath was dry. Enid Pritchard arrived from next door at this point. She turned off the water main tap, but the pools of water continued to form. Finally they called the water company, who promised to send an engineer round. When the water engineer arrived, he soon admitted that he was baffled. He spent a long time checking the pipes, the drains and the taps but he could find nothing wrong. Yet as quickly as the water was mopped up it would reappear. After saying that he would report the problem, he left the house. The water stopped appearing soon after he left.

The next few hours were quiet, but as Phillip and his grandmother were clearing up after supper they heard a clicking noise from the kitchen. They went in to find that the button on the tea dispenser was pushing itself on and off repeatedly, causing tea leaves to cascade over the worktop.

The button continued to operate on its own until the tea ran out. Then it stopped. Seconds later a crash came from the hallway. By now Phillip and his grandmother were thoroughly frightened, but they turned around to see what had caused the sound. The light in the hallway suddenly went on with a loud click. Gingerly venturing into the illuminated space, Phillip discovered that a pot plant had moved from the foot of the stairs to a position halfway up – while the pot in which it usually stood was at the top of the stairs.

Another strange noise now came from the kitchen. A cupboard was rocking back and forth as if an animal were trapped inside. But when Phillip wrenched the door open the movement ceased at once. Totally unnerved by this time, Phillip and Mrs Scholes hastily retreated to Mrs Kelly's house. Called out for the second time that day, Mrs Kelly was now determined to sort things out. She strode over and burst into the kitchen. The cupboard was shaking and rattling again but when she opened it there was nothing there. She checked for hidden wires or strings, but she found none.

Mrs Kelly said that she would stay to make sure nothing else happened. All was quiet after two hours, though, so she went home again. Phillip and his grandmother then went to bed, but no sooner were they under the covers than Phillip's bedroom wardrobe started dancing around his room. The two again fled to Mrs Kelly's house. Mrs Kelly called the police and they arrived within ten minutes. Although the two constables searched the house thoroughly for signs of an intruder or any trickery they found nothing.

Victor Kelly suggested that they should phone a friend named O'Donald, who had an interest in ghosts and the supernatural. O'Donald went straight over to the house with the Kellys when he arrived. It was freezing cold inside, though it was a warm evening outside. They sat in the house for some time but nothing happened. O'Donald filled in the time by explaining how a poltergeist is different from a classic ghost. As they got up to leave, O'Donald told them that poltergeists often returned to the scene of a visitation. Then he added, 'They are very fond of tearing up photographs, I believe.' This is not, in fact, true, but O'Donald had recently been reading about a visitation in which such a thing had happened. As soon as he finished speaking there came a crash. A wedding day photograph of Joe and Jean Pritchard had been knocked over. When Mr Kelly picked it up he saw that the photograph inside the frame had been cut in half. It seems that the poltergeist could hear what O'Donald was saying.

That was the end of the visitation, or so it seemed. For two years nothing untoward happened at all. Phillip left school and went to work with his father, while Mrs Scholes had taken to spending most weekends at the house. Otherwise, things had not changed much in the Pritchard household. It was August when the visitation returned. Jean was taking a break from decorating Diane's bedroom. As she sat drinking tea in the kitchen with her mother, they heard what they described as a 'swooshing noise'. When Jean went to investigate she found the counterpane of her bed at the foot of the stairs. She carried it upstairs, but a crash made her dash back down again. This time Phillip's counterpane was lying in the hallway, together with several upturned pot plants. Mrs Scholes began to cry. 'It is starting again,' she sobbed. Indeed it was.

That night Jean woke up for some reason. Then she saw something moving on the landing. She went out to have a look. As she turned on the light a paint brush flew past her face, followed by a pot of paste. The paste pot struck the wall with such force that it splattered its contents everywhere. At the end of the landing a roll of wallpaper was jigging and dancing about. When Jean stepped forward to grab it, it fell to the floor and lay still. Then the carpet sweeper rose into the air and began to sway about. Jean bolted back to her bedroom, pursued by a roll of wallpaper. Joe was awoken by the fuss, as were Diane and Phillip. All four stood on the landing and watched the sweeper bobbing about in mid-air. A paintbrush was flung at Diane. It hit her on the shoulder, though the blow did not hurt. And then the bizarre events stopped.

An ear-splitting tearing sound drew everyone's attention to Diane's bedroom. The wooden curtain pelmet over the window had been torn off the wall. It hovered for a moment and then it lurched out of the open window to crash into the garden. Joe slammed the door shut, hoping to trap whatever 'it' was in Diane's bedroom. This seemed to work because the door began to shake and rattle as if something were trying to get out. Then silence fell. The family went back to bed. Diane spent the night in her parents' room and they all managed to get some fitful sleep. The poltergeist was back, and it was not going to leave for nine long months.

The visitation soon settled down into a pattern – so much so that the family took to calling the invisible intruder 'Fred'. The poltergeist was mostly active after supper, through to around 1am. It hardly ever did anything during the day, though sometimes ornaments would be found in different places, or even different rooms, from where they had been left. As well as moving objects, the poltergeist specialized in noises. These varied between fairly soft knocks and loud bangs, as if a great drum were being beaten in the room. Sometimes the entire house would shake to the vibrations of the louder thumps, which could be heard up to a hundred yards away. The moving ornaments usually rose into the air and floated around the room for a few seconds before being gently put down. On one occasion a kitchen cupboard opened and dozens of plates and cups floated out, only to be carefully placed on the floor.

Also within the poltergeist's repertoire was the switching on or off of lights. On more than one occasion, it actually switched off the electricity at the mains. It would also tear bedclothes off in the middle of the night. Diane was usually the one who suffered this mishap. It was Diane, too, who was sometimes tipped bodily out of her bed to the floor as the mattress floated upwards. A visitor once made the mistake of saying that she did not believe that there was a poltergeist. The fridge door immediately opened and a jug of milk floated out. As the horrified guest watched the jug of milk threw itself at her, drenching her upper body.

The poltergeist seemed to have a sense of humour, too. It once removed a sandwich from a plate and hid it behind the television. When the sandwich was retrieved it bore the clear impression of a set of gigantic teeth. In another incident a pair of gloves came to life and moved around the house as if they were attached to an invisible person. Less amusing for the family was the occasion on which all of the door handles were smeared with jam. The poltergeist annoyed them further by unwinding rolls of toilet paper and stringing them around the house. Perhaps the most inventive of its tricks, though, was when Jean's white mohair cardigan went missing. It was found some time later in the coal shed. Although it

*The Pontefract poltergeist had a fascination with the fridge and its contents. On one occasion, it emptied a jug full of milk over a guest and it loved to float eggs around the house*

was half-buried in coal it proved to be immaculately clean when it was pulled out, though it should have been covered in black coal dust.

About five months into the visitation the family witnessed a very dramatic demonstration of 'Fred's' power. As they all sat watching TV one evening, an egg floated in from the hallway, hovered briefly and then fell and smashed. A second egg did the same thing. Jean ran to the kitchen to find the fridge door open and two eggs missing. She grabbed the remaining four eggs, put them into a wooden box and sat on it. Despite this precaution a third egg floated into the sitting room and broke on the floor. Jean hurriedly opened the box and peered inside. There were only three eggs left. She shut the box and sat on it again. Eggs floated in and smashed on three more occasions. After the final egg had fallen, Jean opened the box again. All of the eggs had gone, even though the box had been held shut by her body weight. It seemed that Fred could move eggs through solid objects.

At other times the poltergeist seemed to be more sinister than playful. Once when Diane was going up the stairs the temperature suddenly plummeted and an ominous black shadow formed on the wall. The hall stand then rose into the air and moved towards her: she stumbled and fell. It finally came to rest on top of her, pinning her to the stairs in a most uncomfortable fashion. Phillip and Jean ran to her aid, but they could not shift the stand, which seemed to be held in place by some force much stronger than they were. A few minutes later the force vanished and Diane was able to be rescued.

About six months after the visitation began a neighbour told the Pritchards about an old legend that was current in Pontefract. Apparently there had once been a monastery there, but like many others it had been demolished in the 16th century, following the Reformation. According to the tale, one of the monks who had lived in the monastery had been an evil and violent man. His crimes reached a climax when he raped and strangled a local teenage girl. The monk was tried and found guilty. He was then led to the gallows that stood on a hill just outside Pontefract – the hill on which the new housing estate was built. A couple of weeks later 'Fred' was seen for the first time.

Strangely enough, after the Pritchards had been told the story about the monk they began to see him. One night Jean and Joe were in bed. Something woke them up and then the bedroom door swung slowly open. They could see a figure gliding along the landing. It was totally black, it was slightly taller than Joe and it wore a cloak and a hood. The same figure was seen by a neighbour a few days later. A visitor also saw the tall figure in a black robe. Fred began to be called the Black Monk. By this time, the poltergeist seemed to be gaining in power. As became clear later, the visitation was moving towards a climax. The 'Black Monk' began to find a voice. This began as the sound of heavy breathing, which was usually heard at night. Then it began to imitate the sound of a cow or a chicken.

One evening in early May, Diane was walking down the hallway when the lights suddenly went out, leaving her in the dim light of dusk. Then she felt something tugging at the front of her jumper, pulling her towards the stairs. She screamed, which brought Jean and Phillip from the sitting room. By this point the invisible hands had such a firm grip on Diane's clothing that they managed to pull her up the first couple of steps. Jean and Phillip could clearly see the jumper being pulled out in front of Diane, where the invisible hands had a hold. Jean grabbed her daughter around the waist and tried to pull her back down.

The invisible attacker then grabbed Diane around the throat with what felt like an enormously powerful hand. Diane began to choke. Phillip squeezed past his mother and made a lunge forward, in an attempt to make contact with the invisible assailant. Instantly the invisible force vanished and the three humans tumbled into a heap. But there had been no mistake. The red weals on Diane's neck showed where the invisible hand had gripped her.

Three days later Phillip and Diane were relaxing in the sitting room when Phillip glanced up and saw the black-robed figure moving down the hallway. As he got up to follow it, he saw it pass into the kitchen. When it got there it stopped as if it were looking about. Then it began to sink downwards into the floor, before vanishing altogether. The visitation was over as abruptly as it had begun. This case raises some serious issues for those who feel that all poltergeist visitations must have a focus. The first outbreak took place when Phillip and Mrs Scholes were the only people in the house – the rest of the family were away on holiday. Yet the second and much longer visitation seemed to focus on Diane. Neither of the children appear to have been particularly stressed or upset, nor had there been any dramatic changes in the family situation at around the time of either outbreak.

Otherwise, the visitation seemed to play out in true poltergeist fashion. The second stage began with a number of dramatic events, but they were intermittent and spread out.

It was a while before the poltergeist was able to create manifestations on consecutive evenings. The pace and variety of its stunts increased as the months passed, but it was not able to make a sound like a human breathing until the very end of its stay. Nor could it appear as a solid black monk. On this occasion the visitation ended abruptly, which is normal enough, though other visitations have been known to tail off gradually.

## The Tropication Arts Visitation

The following events took place in Miami, Florida, which demonstrates the fact that poltergeist activity does not know any geographical boundaries. In January 1967 paranormal researcher Suzy Smith was being interviewed on WKAT, a local radio station, when they received a phone call from a Tropication Arts employee. The young girl claimed that her workplace was being haunted by a ghost that smashed things. Smith decided to investigate. After obtaining permission she visited the company's warehouse, which was full of trinkets, souvenirs and fancy dress novelties. She discovered that the strange events had begun in the middle of December. Some glass mugs had been found smashed on the floor when the staff had arrived for work. As the days went by the amount of damage increased steadily. By the time Smith became involved about a dozen objects were being broken each day. Typically, an ornament would fall off a shelf and smash on the floor when nobody was near it. Just occasionally an object would shatter into fragments as it sat on the shelf.

One of the owners, Alvin Laubheim, had called the police in soon after Christmas. A sergeant had been searching the warehouse when a beer glass had slid off a shelf and crashed to the floor in front of his eyes. The policeman assumed that it had been pushed from behind by somebody he could not see, so he whipped out his pistol and shouted, 'I'll shoot at the next thing to move!' Within the next few seconds, no fewer than 15 objects flung themselves from the shelves. The sergeant holstered his gun and left hurriedly. Smith called in other investigators to help her. Together they carefully ruled out any normal methods by which the objects could have been moved. Meanwhile, Smith noticed that the damage only occurred when one particular employee, 19-year-old Julio Vasquez, was in the warehouse. When he had a day off, or was out on a delivery, nothing happened. Vasquez denied causing the mayhem, but he did admit that he was unhappy in his job. The trouble ceased abruptly when he left Tropication Arts and got a new job elsewhere.

## The Rosenheim Visitation

The Black Monk of Pontefract had shown that it was able to manipulate modern electric light switches as easily as earlier poltergeists had moved farm tools and ornaments. However, the poltergeist that struck the office of a Bavarian lawyer was to demonstrate a much greater level of technological ability. As is often the case, the visitation began fairly quietly. It was in the autumn of 1967 that Sigmund Adam began to realize that something was wrong. First of all, several telephone calls were cut off in his office at 13 Königstrasse, Rosenheim, Bavaria. Then the phones began to ring when nobody was calling. Finally, all the phones rang at once, which was when Herr Adam called in the engineers. Working in the office at the time were Herr Adam, a manager named Johannes Englehard, two clerks – Gustel Huber and Anne-Marie Schneider – and a part-time junior named Frau Bielmeier.

First on the scene was an engineer from Siemens, who had installed the office equipment. He found nothing wrong, but the malfunctions continued. The engineer returned and again found nothing wrong, but he replaced the telephonic equipment all the same. When the new equipment malfunctioned as well, Siemens suggested that the fault might lie with the external Post Office lines. The Post Office could find nothing wrong either, but they appeared to think that the fault lay with them. They not only replaced the external lines and the telephonic equipment but they also installed a meter that could record all of the calls that came in or went out. On 5 October the meter sprang into life. It recorded an outgoing call even though nobody in the office was on the telephone at the time. Two weeks later the same thing happened. On this second occasion a Dr Schmidt was visiting the office and he signed an account of the event for Herr Adam to show to the Post Office.

The Post Office then produced a log of the calls that had been recorded by the meter over the previous five weeks. According to the log hundreds of calls had been made from the office, many to the same number. In particular, 600 calls had been made to 0119, the speaking clock. Herr Adam and his staff denied making the calls, but the Post Office declared that all the calls that had been recorded were genuine and had been dialled from the Adam office. When they presented Herr Adam with a huge bill, he was furious. He studied the list of calls and discovered that on one particular day the speaking clock had been dialled 46 times in just 15 minutes. Given the mechanical dialling mechanism of the phones in the office, dialling 0119 would take 17 seconds, so it was physically impossible for anyone to dial the clock so often in such a short time. The Post Office would not listen, though. They demanded payment of the bill.

Herr Adam refused to pay so the Post Office took away all of the telephones except one that had a lock on it. Only Herr Adam had a key yet the mystery calls continued to be made. But the telephones were only a start, because the strange manifestations soon escalated. On 20 October all of the lights in the office went out at once. An electrician, Herr Bauer, was called in. He discovered that all of the light bulbs had been unscrewed. It seemed to be just a question of pushing them back into their sockets so that they all worked again. Herr Bauer had just finished packing up when the lights again went out. Just as before, they had all been unscrewed. Puzzled, he put them back. A few days later all of the fuses popped out, cutting off the electricity supply. Herr Bauer sent for the electricity company.

The electricity company sent senior engineer Herr Paul Brunner along. When he arrived on 15 November he checked the wiring throughout the entire building. Although he found nothing wrong he installed meters to record the electricity usage, voltage fluctuations and changes in magnetic fields. He also replaced the fuses with a more robust, screw-in type and then he sealed them shut. Satisfied with his arrangements, he said that he would come back in a couple of weeks to inspect the meters. In the meantime, he asked Herr Adam to call him if anything odd happened. He did not have long to wait.

On 20 November Herr Adam called Herr Brunner, who arrived

*Herr Adam points at one of the paintings that was most affected by the poltergeist*

with a team of engineers and analysts. During the morning the lights had all undone themselves again and a fluorescent tube in Herr Adam's private office had suddenly leapt from its mountings and smashed on the floor. When Brunner checked the meters he discovered that there had been a series of power surges and odd fluctuations. These had occurred only during office hours. The largest surge had taken place when the fluorescent tube had fallen to the floor. Brunner re-seated the meters just to be sure.

Next day Brunner returned to replace the fluorescent tubes with normal light bulbs. While he was there the photocopier began leaking chemicals. On the following day all of the light bulbs blew when a power surge struck. Determined to get to the bottom of the mystery, Brunner arranged for the office to be connected to the local substation by heavy duty cables. The power surges continued, so Brunner assumed that the problems lay with the substation. He moved his team out of Herr Adam's office. They all returned on Monday 27 November having found nothing wrong with the substation. By this time Brunner was running out of ideas, so he disconnected Adam's office from the mains supply and installed a generator. But it changed nothing. During the day all of the light bulbs exploded in turn, showering glass fragments around the office. The generator ran perfectly, but the power surges in the office continued. Next morning it became clear that the problem did not lie with the telephone system or the electricity supply.

The light fittings began swinging wildly from side to side. Watching this, Herr Adam remarked, 'All we need now is for the paintings to move.' Seconds later a painting began to revolve on the wall. It had been hung

*Light fittings in the Rosenheim office swing from side to side, caught on a security camera installed to monitor the situation*

from a nail by a cord, which was found to be wrapped tightly around the nail. Then other paintings began to move. Two of them fell from the wall and crashed to the ground. At that point Herr Brunner concluded his investigations with these words:

> *It is necessary to postulate the existence of a power as yet unknown to science, of which neither the nature nor strength nor direction could be defined. It is an energy beyond comprehension.*

The electricity company called in two physicists, Dr Karger and Dr Zicha, to examine Brunner's records. The physicists also reviewed the reports about the telephonic malfunctions. They concluded that the strange force was not electrical, sonic or magnetic, but they also believed that it was under intelligent control, in view of the way in which it had behaved.

Herr Adam had already told the police that somebody was trying to ruin him by running up huge phone bills and terrifying his staff. When Brunner moved out, Officer Wendl moved in to begin a criminal investigation. Rather than spend time fruitlessly exploring the 'How?' of the problem, Wendl began investigating the 'Who?' and the 'Why?' He began by assuming that somebody had a grudge against Herr Adam and was therefore trying to make things difficult for him. His method of working was to track back through Adam's past legal cases, financial affairs and past and present employees. At first he drew a blank, but then he realized that one of the clerks, 18-year-old Anne-Marie Schneider, was unhappy at work. She apparently blamed Adam for the petty feuds and problems that were affecting her relations with other members of staff.

Wendl went back over the records of the company and found that the assorted disturbances had happened only on the days when Schneider was in the office. On her days off no untoward events had taken place. To see if his suspicions were correct, Wendl asked Adam to give each of his staff a couple of days off. When it came to Schneider's turn the unexplained events ceased abruptly.

Convinced that he had found the culprit, Wendl decided to have Schneider watched. He thought she must be using some sophisticated trickery to cause the events. The days went by and the poltergeist activity continued, but the police watching Schneider were unable to report anything unusual. Then a massive oak cabinet moved across the office while Schneider and Huber were alone together. The cabinet was so heavy that even if Huber were an accomplice, Schneider could not have shifted it. Two policemen struggled to shift it back into place.

Still convinced that Schneider was the cause of the trouble, Wendl presented Adam with his evidence. Adam agreed that it looked very much as if Schneider was to blame, but neither man had the slightest idea of how she was doing it. As a last resort, Hans Bender of the Freiburg Institute of Parapsychology was called in. He persuaded Schneider to spend a few days in Freiburg so that she could undergo a series of ESP (extra-sensory perception) tests. The results proved to be negative – the young woman had no special abilities. Nevertheless, Herr Adam dismissed her from his office. Schneider later moved to Munich and got on with her life. There were no further instances of poltergeist activity, either in Herr Adam's office or around Schneider.

What was noted by researchers at the time was that the Rosenheim

*Anne-Marie Schneider seems to have been the focus for the visitation*

visitation had occurred in a place of work, whereas nearly all previous poltergeist events had been experienced in someone's home. However, many of the earlier events had taken place in homes that were also workplaces, such as farms, pubs and workshops. It seems that the departure might not have been as significant as was thought at the time. The Rosenheim visitation attracted the attention of numerous technicians, scientists and policemen, all of whom admitted to being completely baffled by the events. In terms of poltergeist effects, however, the Rosenheim case was relatively tame. That was very definitely not the case with a visitation that began in 1977 in the north London suburb of Enfield.

## The Harper Visitation

The affected house belonged to the Harper family, which at the time consisted of Mrs Harper, who was divorced, and her four children: Rose aged 13, Janet aged 11, Pete aged ten and Jimmy who was seven. Mrs Harper's brother, John Burcome, lived in the next street. The Harper family got on well with their immediate neighbours, Vic and Peggy Nottingham and their son Gary.

Their house would attract a number of leading researchers and their experiences would prove to be enormously newsworthy. However, there would be accusations of trickery as well as evidence of genuine phenomena.

The visitation began as the children went to bed on the evening of 30 August 1977. Pete and Janet, who shared a bedroom, were the first to experience anything strange. The pair came downstairs only minutes after Mrs Harper had switched the light off. They said their beds had been shaking and shuddering. Mrs Harper went up with them but found nothing amiss, so she ordered them back to bed. The next evening the same two called down to their mother. This time they could hear a funny noise. Mrs Harper went up, switched the light on and listened. She could hear nothing so she assumed that the children were playing a trick on her. But when she switched the light off she immediately heard a strange sound. It was like a man shuffling over a wooden floor while wearing slippers, she said later. Then there came four distinct knocks, like someone rapping their knuckles on a wooden board. She switched the light back on and was astonished to see the chest of drawers sliding across the floor. It moved about 18 inches (45 centimetres) before it stopped. Mrs Harper went over to push it back into position, but it would not move. It was as if some invisible force was pushing it from the other side. 'Right,' Mrs Harper announced, 'everybody downstairs.'

Mrs Harper shepherded the children next door and explained to the Nottingham family what had happened. At this stage they all assumed that there was some intruder in the house. Vic and Gary went back to the Harper household, but when they searched the place thoroughly they found nothing. As they were preparing to leave, the knocking noises began again. They seemed to be coming from inside the walls. Vic searched the gardens, while Gary stayed indoors, following the noises from room to room. At 11pm the Nottinghams gave up trying to find the intruder and called the police. WPC Carolyn Heeps arrived promptly, listened to the story and then ventured into the house. She too searched without finding anything. However, when she entered the living room the knocking noises began again. Heeps stopped to listen, at which point a chair slid across the floor towards her. It moved about three feet (91 centimetres) and then stopped. She left the house, saying that there was nothing she could do about ghosts. After that she went off to file a written report of the incident. This report would prove to be of great importance to investigators because it confirmed that an independent witness had experienced something odd at the earliest stages of the visitation.

The Harpers slept next door that night and then ventured back to their house on the following morning. Everything was normal until marbles and Lego bricks began to be thrown around in the downstairs rooms. Mrs Harper bent down to pick up a marble, but it was too hot to touch and she had to drop it again. After a few minutes the activity stopped, but it repeated itself each evening for four days.

Mrs Harper called the local vicar, but he was unwilling to get involved, so Vic Nottingham telephoned the *Daily Mirror*. He asked them who should be contacted if the police and the Church could not help. On 4 September the *Daily Mirror* sent a reporter, Douglas Bence, and a photographer, Graham Morris. The two stayed for some hours talking to the Harpers without anything strange happening. Then just as the pressmen were preparing to leave a Lego brick levitated. Morris got out his camera to take a shot but while he was focusing he was struck hard on the forehead by another Lego brick. The blow resulted in a bruise that was still visible a week later.

When Bence and Morris reported back to the newspaper, a senior reporter named George Fellows offered to take a hand. He had investigated several alleged ghosts in the past. Although some of them could not be explained, others had been found to have less than psychic origins. Sometimes a pub landlord wanted to get his pub into the newspapers or a teenager was playing a prank. In the case of council house tenants such as the Harpers, Fellows knew that allegations were sometimes made in order to get a better home. So when he went to see the Harpers he asked them if they wanted to move house. Mrs Harper said they were happy where they were, but they just wanted to get rid of their ghost.

Convinced that the Harpers were genuine, Fellows called the Society for Psychical Research and suggested that they should investigate. The SPR contacted a member named Maurice Grosse. Born in 1919, Grosse had served in the army during the Second World War, before founding a successful engineering business. He had a long-standing interest in the paranormal and after his retirement he took up investigating cases and events. Because he lived in north London, the Enfield house was almost on his doorstep.

Grosse made his first visit to the house on the evening of 8 September. He was greeted by a flying marble which had not been thrown by any of the Harper children. A few minutes later, the long brass chimes of the doorbell began to swing back and forth. Then a door slammed shut, flew open and slammed a second time. Later that evening a shirt floated up from a pile of fresh laundry and dropped down to the floor.

Reviewing his notes after getting home, Grosse thought that the most likely focus for the case was Janet. Indeed, he rather suspected her of faking the phenomena. While the others had seemed agitated, upset or frightened, Janet had been quite relaxed about the affair. She was also

*Maurice Grosse of the Society for Psychical Research, who investigated the Enfield case*

in the room each time something odd happened. While Grosse had not caught her doing anything, he decided that he would keep a careful eye on her when he returned. He also intended to search for hidden props and wires.

But although he called several times in the next few days he did not witness anything odd.

On 10 September the *Daily Mirror* printed the story, using the headline 'The House of Strange Happenings'. Next day Grosse, Mrs Harper and Mrs Nottingham were interviewed on a local radio station. The media coverage alerted a highly experienced SPR investigator named Guy Lyon Playfair. He called Grosse and asked if he could join the investigation. Grosse agreed. Over the months that followed, Grosse and Playfair would keep a near constant watch on the house between them. They would record hundreds of incidents of poltergeist activity and they would reach their own conclusions about what was going on.

The visitation lasted for 14 months in all. During that time the most frequent activity was knockings and bangings that seemed to come from the walls. Early in the visitation, Grosse suggested that they should try to communicate with the poltergeist. One evening when it was banging away, Grosse shouted out that he wanted to ask questions and that the answers should be given in the form of one knock for 'no' and two knocks for 'yes'. Did the poltergeist understand? Two knocks indicated that it did.

In the question and answer session that followed the poltergeist indicated that it had formerly lived in the house for 30 years. The poltergeist then fell silent. Another session a few days later produced the information that the poltergeist had left the house 53 years earlier. That would mean that the spirit had taken up residence 83 years before. Grosse knew the house was not that old and asked, 'Are you having a game with me?' At that, a box of cuddly toys lifted up, floated eight feet (2.4 metres) through the air and hit Grosse on the head. Later sessions produced nonsensical answers, so Grosse gave up his attempts at communication. On one visit, Playfair and Grosse noticed that several items of furniture had disappeared from the house. They asked Mrs Harper about this. She said that the items had come from a nearby house, where a child had died in suspicious circumstances. The parents had sold up and left soon afterwards. She was worried that the entity causing the trouble had come into her house with the furniture, so she had got rid of it. For the next few days some of the pillows on the beds displayed small indentations, as if a child had been resting on them. As had so often been the case, it seemed that a poltergeist was acting in line with the expectations of its witnesses.

Then in October 1977 the poltergeist became more active. It had previously confined its efforts to moving toys or sliding furniture across floors. Now it began throwing furniture about. A chair beside Janet's bed came in for a lot of attention – it was regularly flung about. Grosse tried securing it to the leg of the bed with a piece of stout wire. A few hours later the chair had been overturned, and the wire had been broken. Grosse then secured it with several twists of the same wire. The chair was again found overturned and the wire was broken a short time later. Rather more dramatic was the fate of the gas fire, a heavy metal contraption that was cemented into the living room wall. One day the family came home to find that it had been torn from the wall and dragged across the room towards the doorway. After that, the furniture began to be moved about more and more often. It was left in ever more bizarre places. The front door could not be opened one day because a bed had been pushed up against it. Then the younger children began to complain that they could see the face of an old man hovering about, though nobody else saw this.

Increasingly, the events were starting to centre on Janet. She was tipped out of chairs and thrown out of bed and she fell into trances. Finally, in late November, a strange dog-like barking noise began to be heard. It was only evident when Janet was present, but it did not seem to come from her. Over the course of the next few days the bark became a whistle, and then a gasp and finally a harsh male voice. When Grosse and Playfair questioned the voice, it claimed to be two distinct people. The first person was a man called Joe Watson. This was the name of the man who had lived in the house before the Harpers. He had died after suffering a massive throat haemorrhage while sleeping in a chair in the living room. When the voice was claiming to be Watson, it usually uttered a stream of obscenities and made meaningless comments.

The second identity claimed by the voice was that of someone called Bill Haylock. 'Bill' claimed that he was buried in the nearby Durants Park cemetery. He had come to the house looking for his family, he said, 'but they are not here now'. The voice would often ramble on when it claimed to be Bill. It demanded that jazz music be put on the radio and it told people to leave the house. Asked why he was bothering the Harpers, 'Bill' replied, 'I like annoying you.' Many other poltergeists have explained their motives in this way. When Rose asked 'Bill' why he did not move on to where the dead people went, the voice responded rather sadly, 'I am not a heaven man.'

Oddly, 'Bill's' account of his death exactly mirrored the circumstances of the real Joe Watson's last hours. Events were clearly building up to something of a climax as November came to an end. The peak of activity was reached on 15 December. As well as the usual mayhem of flying ornaments, wandering furniture and loud noises, Janet claimed that she had been levitated in her bedroom. This was a memorable day for Janet in another way, too. It marked the beginning of her first period. The level of poltergeist activity diminished rapidly after this time.

In the spring of 1978 the manifestations began to increase again. This time they were of a rather different kind, though – they rarely happened when anyone was present. Instead, furniture and ornaments quietly moved around in empty rooms. When a new investigator arrived at the Enfield house, she could find no evidence of genuine paranormal activities. She quickly formed the opinion that Janet and Rose were faking the apparent phenomena.

In a radio interview that she gave a few years later, Janet admitted that she and Rose had indeed faked the later phenomena. She insisted, however, that the earlier manifestations had been genuine. Some sceptics chose to believe that her confession meant that the sisters had been tricking Grosse and Playfair from the start. Other researchers gave them the benefit of the doubt.

## The Role of the Human Environment

Numerous other poltergeists have been seen in recent years, but little would be gained by examining all of the accounts in detail. The studies carried out by earlier researchers have generally confirmed the usual pattern of poltergeist visitations.

However, some of the more recent investigations have established the importance of the human environment in which the visitations have taken place. This aspect of poltergeist activity was mostly absent from earlier reports. Whether the events have taken place at work or at home, it has usually been the case that people have been surrounded by tension, frustration or even unhappiness. There does not seem to have been outright hostility between antagonists. It is often more of a low-level, simmering discontent. Focus people are usually teenagers and they are more often girls than boys – but that does not seem to be an iron rule. Teenage girls often appear to be associated with the more dramatic events, which is perhaps why they are noticed. On the other hand, young men and teenage boys seem to be more often involved with the less sensational manifestations.

These aspects, and others, must be considered when one is attempting to understand, analyse and explain poltergeist visitations. But before doing so, one other feature of the poltergeist phenomenon must be looked at. In some ways it is the oddest feature of all. Poltergeist activity does not always take place when a visitation is in progress. It can occur in a number of other scenarios as well. It is time to look at them.

# chapter 7

# PHANTOM NUDGERS & OTHER PHYSICAL HAUNTINGS

Many studies of the poltergeist phenomenon concentrate on full-blown visitations, but in a vast number of incidents only one or two features of a visitation are present. A general pattern is not established.

Very often those on the receiving end of these events do not recognize that a poltergeist-like event is in progress, so they look for other explanations. It is not always easy to determine if a poltergeist is involved or if something else is going on.

## The 'Flying Peaches of Shreveport'

Take for instance the case of the 'flying peaches of Shreveport' which occurred on 12 July 1961. Three builders were repairing the roof of a house in Shreveport, Louisiana when they were bombarded by a hail of what they took to be golf balls. The objects were small and round and they hurt when they collided with anybody. Annoyed by the intrusion, the builders looked around expecting to see a gang of teenagers throwing missiles – but they could see nobody. The balls seemed to be falling vertically down from a cloudy sky. Thoroughly mystified, the builders retreated from the roof and took shelter while the bombardment continued. After about five minutes the workmen ventured out. They soon discovered that what they had taken for golf balls were, in fact, unripe peaches. The builders picked up around 200 of the green and hard fruits.

When they reported the incident to the police, it was suggested that the peaches had been scooped up from a nearby orchard by a strong gust of wind. The story got into the local press, and a reporter contacted the United States Weather Bureau for an explanation. However, the organization could not come up with an answer. After studying the weather charts for Shreveport on the day concerned they announced that it had been a calm, normal day. Only something like a mini-tornado

*Builders working on the roof of a house in Shreveport, Louisiana, were assaulted on 12 July 1961 by a barrage of peaches that seemed to come out of nowhere*

could have lifted 200 peaches into the sky – and there was no record of such an event. Again the single shower of peaches was all that occurred. The phenomenon did not progress into a poltergeist visitation.

## A Shower of Hazelnuts

A similar event took place on 13 March 1977 in Bristol. This time, though, it echoed a feature of the Bell Witch visitation. Alfred Osborne and his wife were walking home from a Sunday morning church service when they heard a clicking noise. It came from the pavement in front of them. Thinking that a button had come off his coat, Mr Osborne looked down at the ground in front of him. All he could see was a hazelnut. A second or two later another hazelnut fell on to the pavement. Mr and Mrs Osborne looked around, expecting to discover that the nuts had been thrown by a child or a prankster. In that same instant, the two stray hazelnuts had turned into a deluge. Hazelnuts were falling vertically from the sky. About a thousand nuts fell in less than 30 seconds and then the shower abruptly ceased.

'They were coming from the sky, from a considerable height,' Mr Osborne told a reporter from the local newspaper later that day. 'They were peppering all around on the road, bouncing off cars and rolling in the gutters.' Mr Osborne offered the reporter one of the hundreds of nuts that he had picked up. It was fresh and sweet. The reporter suggested that a gust of wind had picked the nuts up from a local wood. Mr Osborne was contemptuous of the idea. 'I don't know where you could suck up hazelnuts in March,' he said. 'They don't ripen until late summer.' It will be recalled that the Bell Witch deposited a large number of fresh hazelnuts, equally out of season, on Mrs Bell's bed when she was ill one time.

## When It Rained Seeds

A couple of years later there came another curious shower. It was not hazelnuts this time but seeds – hundreds of thousands of them. On 12 February 1979, Ronald Moody was alone in his sitting room in Southampton when he heard a strange 'rushing sound' coming from his conservatory. When he went through to investigate, the room was strangely dark – the glass roof was entirely covered by a mass of tiny seeds. Stepping outside, Mr Moody saw that it was literally raining seeds. Thousands of tiny, pale brown seeds were cascading down from directly above. The shower stopped almost immediately. Mr Moody guessed that the seeds were ordinary cress seeds – as indeed they proved to be when he tried growing some later on – but their sheer number was astonishing. He counted 500 seeds in a space that was only six inches (15 centimetres) square. The seeds covered his entire back garden, his conservatory and parts of his neighbour's garden as well.

Deeply puzzled, Mr Moody collected up some of the seeds. He then went inside to phone a friend, but at that point he heard another 'whooshing noise'. His garden was now being engulfed by mustard seeds. The sky was black with them. As before, the torrent quickly stopped. In the two hours that followed vast quantities of everyday seeds fell from the sky on five separate occasions. This event reads very much like the opening salvo of the Battersea House of Mystery affair, but nothing further happened. The strange rain of seeds came out of an unremarkable sky. It was accompanied by snow flurries. All of the seeds fell on one day and that was the end of the affair.

## The Haunting of the Brushmakers Arms

Showers of anomalous objects are frequently found in poltergeist visitations, but isolated deluges may or may not be psychic phenomena. However, some incidents feature a wider range of poltergeist-like events. Take, for instance, the haunting of the Brushmakers Arms at Upham, Hampshire. The public house takes its name from the fact that the original building was constructed as part-house, part-brush factory.

About 400 years ago a murder took place there. The victim was Mr Chickett, for whom the original building was constructed. As he grew older, his fortune grew greater. He would sit upstairs in his bedroom counting out his gold and silver coins, before concealing them in a hidden compartment. It was not, however, hidden well enough. One morning his workers arrived to find their employer battered to death, with his room ransacked and his money stolen.

After such a heinous crime Mr Chickett's spirit could not rest easy. Four centuries later it appears that he has still not left the scene of his murder. A witness to the physical manifestations recalls his experience:

> *Saw it myself in here. A few years back now. I was sitting at the bar, about where you are, when the bottles started moving. Two of them fell off the*

*shelf on to the floor. Then one flew across the bar. It was like someone was throwing it, but it didn't break. Just shot across the room and landed on that table there by the window.*

The distance indicated was about 15 feet (4.5 metres). Glasses, bottles and other objects are moved around the bar about once a month, though it is unusual for anyone to see them move.

Just as often, footsteps are heard moving out of the room in which the murder took place. They go along the corridor and down the stairs and then they stop in the hall. Rather less frequently the sound of chinking coins is heard from the same small room. The ghost himself is seen only rarely. In 2002, Jill the landlady recalled:

*Last time was about three years ago. I was upstairs doing some paperwork in the office. Suddenly I heard the door to the front bedroom* [where the murder was committed] *slam shut, very hard and loud. I looked round and there was the outline of a man, like a shadow on the wall, moving off. Only it couldn't be a shadow as the sun was not out. And it was not a shadow on the wall, not as such. It was more like a shadow in the middle of the corridor – oh, I am not explaining it very well. It was definitely a man moving down the corridor. Mind you, we haven't seen him since. People hear him of course. But I think he must like us. We get no trouble.*

Here, we can see quite a wide range of poltergeist activity: noises, objects moving and a sinister black shape. Other elements are missing, no knocks or voices and the only objects to be moved around are small and light.

The level of activity is very low, with an inexplicable event happening only once or twice a month, rather than several times a day as is more typical.

What really makes this case different from a more usual visitation is that the activity has been going on for at least 50 years. There are locals in the village who can remember the strange activity at the pub as far back as the 1950s – and they say that it was nothing new then. Maybe the activity really has been going on since the time of the murder. This long period of time would seem to rule out the possibility of a focus person. The landlord of the pub has changed at least six times since the 1950s, while staff come and go even more frequently.

## The Haunting of the Crown Inn at Lea

A similar situation exists at the Crown Inn at Lea, Herefordshire. It became a pub when two houses were knocked together in about 1930. The activity in this building is restricted to the downstairs back room, which was formerly the kitchen of the more western of the two houses. It now forms part of the restaurant area of the pub. In particular, the manifestations centre on the rear window that overlooks the pub garden.

Those who have encountered the ghost say that he sits quietly on an equally spectral chair, looking out of the window. He is never seen, but he can be clearly sensed. There is little doubt about his general appearance. Those who have sensed it are very definite about the fact that he is an elderly man. On the whole, this spirit – if such it is – is no trouble at all. He will be sensed now and then by members of staff, but those who have worked here for any amount of time have learned to ignore him. But there are times when the old boy seems to get quite irate. That is when anything is placed where he likes to sit. Then a range of poltergeist-like activity will break out.

In 2005 a new member of staff was given the task of putting up the Christmas decorations. She thought that an empty spot next to a window would make an ideal location for a Christmas tree. So she set up the festive tree and went to work decorating it. The job was finished to her satisfaction so she went off to make a cup of tea. She had only taken a couple of steps into the kitchen when there was an almighty crash from the restaurant area. Hurriedly returning, she saw that the Christmas tree had been overturned and all of her carefully arranged baubles were scattered over the floor. The landlady quickly put her right and advised her to place the tree elsewhere. She did so and no further mishaps occurred.

It is, of course, usually customers who are new to the pub who interfere with the window space. They may move a chair to the area, or leave a drink on the window sill. Inevitably the drink will be overturned or the chair will be moved. On at least one occasion a person unwary enough to sit at the window has been nudged or pinched by some invisible hand.

'Phantom nudgers' have been recognized as a separate category of ghost by some researchers. They frequent public places, such as pubs or railway stations, where they creep up on perfectly unsuspecting humans before delivering a nudge, a shove or a pinch. Always invisible, they persist in their activities for years on end.

# The Philip Experiment

Another outbreak of poltergeist-type activity occurred in Canada in the early 1970s. It took place in the most unusual of circumstances. The train of events began in 1972, when Dr George Owen of the Toronto Society for Psychical Research decided to test the theory: 'Ghosts have an objective reality but they are created out of the minds of those who see them.' In effect, a ghost will appear and will haunt a particular place if enough people believe that it will do so. A 'ghost' is effectively a hallucination projected by those who believe in it. It can be picked up by other people, whether they share that belief or not.

In order to test the idea, Owen recruited a group of seven volunteers who agreed to meet once a week. They would concentrate on an invented ghost in order to see if they could make him appear. Owen created the basic character, though the group collectively wrote his life story in the hope that this would increase the strength of their belief in him.

The character they invented was named Philip. He was imagined to have lived in Diddington, Warwickshire, during the mid-17th century. Philip was a fairly wealthy landowner who had married young for money. His marriage to Dorothea was unhappy, though, so he had embarked on a passionate affair with a beautiful gypsy girl named Margo. Tragedy struck after some months of wild abandon with his tempestuous lover. Dorothea discovered the affair and denounced Margo as a witch. Philip's wife fabricated enough evidence to have Margo convicted and Philip did nothing to save her. He was afraid that he would be accused in his turn. Margo was then burned at the stake, sending Philip into a deep

*Dr George Owen of Toronto, who organized an investigation which would become known as the Philip Experiment and which may offer clues as to the true nature of poltergeists*

depression that resulted in his suicide. The group drew pictures of Philip so that they could visualize what his ghost should look like.

It was felt that this dramatic, romantic and ultimately tragic story was just the sort of thing that should lead to a haunting. The group began to meet regularly. They sat around a table to discuss Philip's life story, they added details and they concentrated hard on the existence of his ghost. When one of the group visited England he made a point of travelling to Diddington, so that he could take photographs of the church and other old buildings. It might create a link to Philip. Nothing happened – the ghost of Philip did not appear.

Then one of the group found a report written for the British Society of Psychical Research by DW Hunt and KJ Bachelor in the 1960s. It described an investigation into the old 19th-century parlour game of table turning. The investigators had apparently been very successful in their efforts to produce phenomena. There were some guidelines for anyone who wanted to repeat their experiment:

> *Nobody must feel responsible for, or pressured into making, phenomena happen; everyone taking part must believe in paranormal events being possible; no surprise should be shown or, if possible, felt when something does happen; a light-hearted, jocular atmosphere should be encouraged.*

The Philip group decided to adopt these guidelines in the hope of getting the spectral Philip to appear to them. They cracked jokes, swapped banter about Philip and his amorous exploits and chatted about their own lives while they were waiting for the ghost of Philip to appear. After barely a month something happened. A ghost did not materialize, but the table vibrated. At first the tremors were light and uncertain, then they gathered in strength over a matter of weeks until the table was juddering and rocking from side to side quite visibly. There was still no ghost, but then one of the members had a thought. 'I wonder if by chance Philip is doing this?' she asked. There was a single loud knock on the table.

It was decided to call out questions to the invisible knocker. They began by instructing it to give one knock for 'yes' and two knocks for 'no'.

It was 'Philip' himself who devised a signal to indicate that he either did not know the answer or he refused to give it. This signal was a scratching sound. Each session would begin with the group members calling out, 'Hello, Philip,' in turn. As they spoke, each person was rewarded with a knock on the table in front of them. When they said, 'Goodbye, Philip,' at the close of each session each person again got a personal knock on the table. When the group began to question the knocker, the invisible entity at once identified itself as Philip. In answer to a series of questions 'Philip' gave a version of his life and death that tallied exactly with that which had been invented by the group. When the group asked questions about things that they had not included in their fictitious background for Philip, the knocker would give clear and direct answers. These answers were always internally consistent with the invented story, but they were not always historically accurate. Interestingly, the historic errors were not known to any of the group at the time. They came to light only when research was carried out into 'Philip's' claims.

As the weeks passed by the knocks got louder and more definite. Owen went to great pains to ensure that no one in his group was indulging in trickery. He checked the table over before and after each session, he frisked the group members and he kept a look out for any tricks. But he never found any.

Each of the group members was asked to keep their hands fully in view of the others, preferably letting them rest on top of the table. By late 1973 the meetings began to get much livelier as 'Philip' began to display the sort of tricks that were common among poltergeists. The table began to bounce up and down – it rose several inches into the air before falling back down again.

When asked to do so, 'Philip' would cause the lights to flicker. Eventually the table took on a life of its own – it danced around the room and floated up into the air. On one occasion it became stuck in the doorway as it tried to escape the room. It sometimes did this even when not a single member of the group was touching it. This ruled out any chance that a group member might be pushing it about, even unconsciously.

In the early months of 1974 the group decided that it was time to carry out some tests. They recorded the knocks, along with the sounds of themselves knocking on the table, and had them analysed. Although the knocks seemed natural to the human ear, they had an unusual sound profile. Knocks produced by human hands began loudly and then died away gradually, as the vibrating wood became still. On the other hand 'Philip's' knocks began loudly and then dropped off to silence very quickly. Then the group decided to try taking movie film of the events. 'Philip' did not seem to mind.

The raps, knocks and table movements all happened as frequently as before – and all was caught on film. Later the group moved the table into a TV studio, where the bizarre events were recorded as a moving TV image.

The Philip group concluded that their attempt to create a visual ghost of Philip had resulted in an auditory ghost instead. However, the experienced poltergeist researcher will have realized that many of 'Philip's' antics are typical of a poltergeist visitation. In particular, a poltergeist will usually claim to be whatever its human observers believe it to be. It could be a witch, a demon or an invented ghost called Philip.

## The Skippy Experiment

Since the Philip Experiment became public there have been several attempts to replicate its success. One of the most productive of these imitations has been the Skippy Experiment – a series of ongoing sessions in Sydney, Australia. The Australian team closely followed the methods of the Philip team. They created a sensational life history for their invented ghost and then they hoped for poltergeist activity.

The Australians invented a teenage girl named Skippy Cartman who entered into a passionate but illicit love affair that resulted in her pregnancy. Her tragic tale ended when she was murdered by the father of the unborn baby. So far the team have heard some soft rapping and scratching noises while they have been sitting around their table. However, none of the more dramatic table-moving events have yet been replicated.

It can be seen that the range of manifestations that are generally associated with poltergeist visitations are not confined to those events.

Some of the features of a visitation can be observed in a range of other situations: conventional hauntings, showers of anomalous objects and entirely invented experiments. Whether this indicates the origin of the poltergeist phenomenon or merely serves to cloud and confuse the issue depends on the viewpoint of the investigator.

It is time to turn to the explanations that have been put forward for the existence of poltergeists. We will be looking at the different viewpoints of researchers, be they sceptics or believers.

# chapter 8

# THEORIES & EXPLANATIONS

Having surveyed the poltergeist phenomenon in its many and varied guises it is time to draw some conclusions. From the cases studied so far in this book it will be apparent that poltergeist visitations can be varied and diverse or they can follow a common pattern.

## The Stages of a Poltergeist Visitation

A hypothetical idealized poltergeist visitation would follow a set course, though it should be noted that any visitation might end at any point during this progression of stages.

## Stage One: Beginnings

A poltergeist visit usually begins with low-volume household noises. Before the Second World War people usually assumed that these noises were made by mice and rats, or any other animals that had found their way into the house. This was probably because such animals did sometimes get into houses in those days. These days we are more likely to interpret such noises as air-locks in the central heating or malfunctions in electrical equipment. Very typical of this first phase is scratching, as if an animal is clawing at a door or a wall. The sound of scratching can at times be abnormally loud, though, far louder than any dog or rat could possibly produce.

During this stage most witnesses are not aware that anything odd or unusual is happening. They typically believe that there is some mundane explanation for the noises. Plumbers, electricians or pest-control experts are called in, but they find nothing that can explain the sounds. The noises continue, despite all efforts to discover their source. They will increase in volume, variety and frequency as time passes.

## Stage Two: Noises

Once the occupants of the building have become accustomed to a variety of apparently normal noises, the visitation moves on to a series of noises that are quite clearly not normal. The most characteristic of these is usually described as a knock or a rap. It is frequently likened to the sound of human knuckles knocking on wood. This sound comes from walls, furniture, doors and other objects around the house. In the Ballechin

House visitation two men heard it coming from the same door when they were on opposite sides of it. Both men assumed that the cause of the knocking was on the other side of the door from themselves, when obviously it was not. In the Cock Lane visitation, the knocking sounded as if it was coming from behind the wooden panelling that lined the rooms – that is, from within the walls. Sometimes the surface that is being knocked can be felt to vibrate, just as if it really has been rapped by knuckles. In other instances this vibration is not present.

In addition to the knocking, other noises are frequently recorded. Some of these may well be variations on the knock. There can be the sound of a cricket ball bouncing on the floor, for instance, or clapping. The sound of cracking also seems to be common – some have compared it to dry wood being snapped in half. Bangs and explosions are heard less frequently, but they can be extremely loud. In the Amherst visitation the witnesses thought that a cannon had been fired just outside the house – they ran out to look for it.

In the Battersea Mystery House case, the crowds in the street could hear the bangs and thumps quite clearly up to 150 yards (137 metres) away. The timing of the inexplicable noises is interesting. They often manifest themselves in the evening. In the case of the mill at Appleby, the noises always came during, or just after, the family ate supper. In the case of the Fox sisters the noises began when the girls went to bed. At Ballechin they began at around midnight. In a country house of the period that would have been when most of the people in the house went to bed. The lower-key noises of *Stage One* are often heard at night, too. Once the noises have become an established part of the visitation they often, but not always, abandon their evening timing. They may then be heard at any time of day or night.

In those visitations where the first stage is missed out, the events will start at *Stage Two*, but only if the male head of the household is away. The Demon Drummer of Tedworth visitation began in truly spectacular fashion when Mr Mompesson was away on business. Many other visitations show a similar pattern.

## Stage Three: Moving Objects

Once the repertoire of noises has been established, the poltergeist may get busy moving objects about. This stage will sometimes begin concurrently with Stage Two.

Rather more dramatic is the throwing of stones. Stone throwing is such a common feature of poltergeist visitations that a name has been coined for the manifestation: lithobolia. The frequency, scale and violence of stone throwing may vary considerably. At the Appleby mill only two stones were thrown, but they were large and heavy and they caused considerable damage. At the Battersea Mystery House hundreds of stones were thrown and again they caused a lot of damage. One feature shared by all outbreaks of lithobolia is that the poltergeist uses stones that are readily to hand. The stones at Appleby quite obviously came from the riverbed outside while those at Battersea were pieces of coal, probably from the family coal shed.

Although stones are usually the most noticeable objects to be moved, the poltergeist seems to be able to move almost anything. At first smaller household objects are moved about.

Ornaments and utensils are the usual choice – they are very often found in the wrong place. In a number of instances the objects are moved so that they are placed very carefully indeed. In one case in Hertfordshire in the 1990s a china duck ornament was moved repeatedly so that it sat on the floor facing directly towards the door. It would then be looking at anybody who walked into the room. Other objects are placed exactly in the middle of a table, or teetering on its edge.

The majority of poltergeists are not so fastidious. They apparently prefer to throw objects about more or less at random. Some poltergeists seem to develop a fixation with one particular object, or type of object. It may be that a particular ornament will be moved day after day. In the Black Monk of Pontefract visitation it was a candlestick that came in for the most frequent moves.

It is rare to see a moving object. More often than not objects move when nobody is around to see them. However, witnesses who have seen an object being moved often say that it looks as if some invisible person has picked it up and carried it at a walking pace. This 'invisible carrier' description is also consistent with what happens when the item is put down. Sometimes objects are put down carefully, but at other times they are dropped. The wine bottles in the Turin wine bar that was investigated by Professor Lombroso would float gently through the air and then fall suddenly. They usually smashed on the hard floor. Conversely, the objects that were moved about in the Sunderland household of Dr Wilkins were always placed very carefully and neatly, without anything breaking. Sometimes, but not always, these objects are warm or even hot when they are picked up.

### Stage Four: Apports and Disapports

On rare occasions objects are not just moved – they appear from nowhere. These are known as 'apports'. Objects that disappear into oblivion are termed 'disapports'. Not many poltergeist visitations reach this level of activity, but the effect can be dramatic.

In the Bell Witch visitation apports happened on at least three occasions. Hazelnuts were brought shelled and then unshelled to Mrs Bell. Then Betsy was presented with a basket of tropical fruit. There may be a crossover between apports and moving objects. In the Pontefract case eggs were moved from the kitchen to the sitting room by the poltergeist, where they were dropped and smashed. However, the eggs had started their journey from inside a sealed wooden box, which was kept shut by one of the witnesses sitting on it. The poltergeist was apparently moving the eggs through solid wood. That is, it was disapporting them from the box and apporting them in the living room. Perhaps all apports are actually being transported from somewhere rather than being created out of thin air.

### Stage Five: Communication

Some poltergeists are capable of communicating with the humans that they are infesting. In the majority of cases the communication is by means of raps and knocks in accordance with a code. Such communication only begins if it is initiated by humans. After instructing a poltergeist to answer with a different number of raps or scratches to indicate 'yes', 'no' or 'don't know', humans then proceed to ask questions. The poltergeists at the convent of St Pierre de Lyon and at Amherst seem typical of those spirits who use such forms of communication. Most instances of communication remain at a basic level, but the Fox sisters seem to have been almost unique in having devised an alphabetical code. This allowed their poltergeist to spell out names and words, thus facilitating a rather more complex series of messages.

Rather fewer poltergeists appear to have gained the ability to speak directly. The voices seemingly come from thin air and are usually described as being disembodied or phantom. Typically, the ability to speak is acquired gradually by the poltergeist. In the case of Gef on the Isle of Man, the speech began with barks and whistles. The Bell Witch began with slurping sounds and a noise akin to the smacking of lips. These noises progress on to mutterings or whisperings, where the sounds of human voices can be discerned but actual words cannot be distinguished. Then the voice will begin to enunciate audible words – but its tone is still rather odd. Earlier observers have often said that the voice is gruff, cracked or stilted. A more modern witness has described the voice as being robot-like. Finally the voice will become more like that of a normal human. It becomes perfectly audible, with a range of tones that is able to convey emotion. It is as if the poltergeist has been slowly learning how to talk by a process of trial and error.

Whether the means of communication is coded knocking or a disembodied voice, poltergeist utterances have a lot in common. The desire to shock is apparent. Poltergeists will often use swear words; or they will insult people or make outrageous allegations. Most of the allegations are false, but some are apparently lifted from local gossip about a person's private life. Poltergeists also seem to know a lot about what is going on in the vicinity. Both Gef and the Bell Witch would repeat things that had been said by a member of the family when they had been well away from the house. The Irvings assumed that Gef had scampered off to follow the person, before hiding in the place where the conversation had taken place; the Bells imagined that their witch could travel far and wide invisibly, in order to spy on them.

A poltergeist's statements about itself usually follow a set pattern. Most noticeably the poltergeist will often make a claim that fits in with how it is being viewed by humans. Gef said he was a mongoose after the Irvings had become convinced that he was a small animal; the Fox sisters' poltergeist claimed that it was the ghost of a man after the girls had said that the noises were caused by a ghost; and the poltergeist at the convent of St Pierre de Lyon claimed to be the spirit of Alix de Telieux only after a nun had suggested that this might be the case. When asked why it is causing such a nuisance, a poltergeist will typically reply that it is doing so for sport, for a joke or for fun. The response is almost universal when the question is put.

Another feature of the claims made by poltergeists about themselves is that they are almost uniformly sensational, exciting and salacious. The poltergeist claiming to be Alix de Telieux seemed to delight in regaling the nuns with tales of Alix's debauched sexual escapades, while the Cock Lane poltergeist claimed that it was the spirit of a woman who had been murdered by her husband. Claims of murder are common among poltergeists, as are tales of crimes, immoral behaviour and daring deeds. If poltergeists are to be believed then none of them are humans who have led routine lives of normal activity. They have either perpetrated the most appalling and outrageous crimes or they have been victims.

When the claims made by poltergeists are checked out, they usually turn out to be false. If they are true, the claims relate to events that are generally fairly well known in the area. It is extremely rare for a poltergeist to be in possession of any information that is not already known to its human witnesses.

### Stage Six: Climax

After a poltergeist case has built up gradually over a period of time there will often be a sudden and distinct increase in the level and frequency of activity. Typically, it will increase even further for a day or two, until a climax is reached. For a few hours the level of activity will be far greater than it has ever been. Then it will drop off rapidly, returning to the level it was at before the climax began. When the poltergeist is communicating with its human witnesses it might announce that it is going to leave. Sometimes it might even set a date and time for its departure. These announcements, unlike most other statements made by poltergeists, generally turn out to be accurate.

### Stage Seven: Decline

As we have seen, after the climax of the visitation has been reached activity will tail off and then cease. Sometimes this will be immediate, or nearly so. In other instances the decline might be spread over several days. During this phase it is usual for the various types of activity to continue much as before, but with increasingly less frequency and violence. Sometimes, but not always, the poltergeist will follow a process that is the reverse of its build-up. First it will lose its voice and then it will lose the ability to move objects. Finally, it will cease making noises at all. The decline is almost always much shorter than the build-up.

### Stage Eight: Endings

The majority of poltergeist visitations simply peter out as the decline nears its conclusion. A few end rather more spectacularly. The Bell Witch visitation, for instance, went out with a bang. A gigantic ball of smoke erupted from the fireplace and exploded loudly and then the voice declared that it was leaving. However, some poltergeist visitations are brought to an end by humans. The visitation that plagued Miss Sharpe at Bethony ended temporarily when the local vicar carried out a prayer service in the house. Although the activity later began again at a lesser level, a second prayer service was enough to end the visitation completely. Other clergymen have been far less successful. Some poltergeists have thrown objects at them while they have been conducting services.

A good number of poltergeist visitations end abruptly when there is a change in someone's personal circumstances. The visitation that affected the offices of Sigmund Adam at Rosenheim ceased instantly when the clerk Anne-Marie Schneider was dismissed.

The poltergeist neither returned to the offices nor to Anne-Marie. Similarly, the Battersea Mystery House visitation ended when Mr

Robinson's teenage nephew went to stay with relatives in the country. These, and other cases, would indicate that poltergeist manifestations are activated by the presence of a particular human in a particular place.

As well as this progression of stages, an idealized poltergeist visitation would incorporate some other features.

## Features of a Poltergeist Visitation

### Focus person

In all of the cases that have been studied in the past few decades, it has been clear to researchers that one particular person is often at the centre of a visitation. Manifestations will occur more frequently when that person is present. They might not even take place if the person is not there. The visitation usually commences in the bedroom that is used by that person. Or it might be connected with a favourite possession of theirs. In poltergeist cases from past centuries, it is often easy to see that a focus person was at the centre of the disturbances. Someone like Elizabeth Parsons, for instance, who featured strongly in the Cock Lane Ghost affair. On some occasions a focus person cannot be identified in a past case. However, it might be fair to assume that those who wrote down the account were so busy trying to identify a witch or a ghost that they simply did not notice something that would have been obvious to a modern researcher.

The focus is very often a teenager or a young adult and it seems to be a girl more often than a boy. This is not always the case, though. Grown adults are sometimes found to be the focus – sometimes even retired folk. Indeed, the general presumption that the focus is always a teenager can sometimes mislead the researcher. In the case of the poltergeist that afflicted the house of Dr and Mrs Wilkins in Sunderland, Harry Price assumed that the focus was the newly married teenage daughter Olive. But she was never present when the manifestations took place while her mother usually was. Perhaps it was Mrs Wilkins who was the focus, not her daughter.

In most cases it is clear that people are not always aware that they are the focus of a visitation. Most families believe that it is just their house that is being haunted, not themselves. If focus people eventually realize that they are somehow related to the visitation, they are both puzzled and distressed by the fact. When Ann Kidner was found close to a burning hayrick she was sobbing almost hysterically. She repeatedly said that she was not responsible. Similarly Virginia Campbell was obviously distressed and upset when her teacher's desk levitated at her school. She broke down and sobbed, 'I'm not doing it, Miss. Please, Miss. Honest I'm not.' Whatever role a focus plays in a manifestation, it would seem that on most occasions it is unconscious. Some focus persons, on the other hand, almost seem to enjoy events. Janet Harper, who was at the centre of the Enfield visitation, seems to have fallen into this category.

## Emotional turmoil

It is often said that focus people are usually in a stressful situation of some kind. The clerk Anne-Marie Schneider did not enjoy her job and she had a grudge against her employer; Esther Cox had just experienced an attempted rape; and Virginia Campbell had suffered the trauma of her parents' divorce before being forced to move from Ireland to Scotland, where she had to share a cramped bedroom with a cousin. Focus people are not always obviously distressed by their situation, but there is usually some sign of underlying worry or frustration.

The type of raw emotion that has just been described does not have to be confined to the focus. It is often felt by all or most of those in the affected household or workplace. Indeed, it is sometimes the case that focus people are not only the centre of the poltergeist activity, but they are also the cause of the emotional problems. Or at least other humans in the vicinity might think so.

## Explanations for the Poltergeist Phenomenon

There are six different explanations for the poltergeist phenomenon. Each has its merits and its problems. They will be dealt with in some detail below, but in outline they are as follows:

1. ***Fraud*** – the supposedly paranormal events are faked by humans.
2. ***Mistake*** – the supposedly paranormal events are entirely natural occurrences that are falsely assumed to be paranormal.
3. ***Entity*** – the events are truly paranormal and are caused by a supernatural entity such as a ghost, a demon or a spirit.
4. ***Repeated Spontaneous Psychokinesis (RSPK)*** – the events are truly paranormal and are caused by the subconscious use of psychokinesis by one or more of the humans involved.

**5.** A combination of two or more of the above.

**6.** Something else as yet unknown to humanity.

In the remainder of this chapter I will compare these suggested explanations with the recorded events.

Fraud or fakery is often alleged in poltergeist outbreaks. It is certainly true that a proportion of those who have reported a visitation have been found to be faking some or all of the events. Elizabeth Parsons was most certainly faking the later manifestations of the Cock Lane Ghost and Janet Harper admitted faking some of the Enfield events. Whether either girl had faked the earlier manifestations in either case is open to doubt. Parsons was caught faking the knocking noises only after other witnesses had reported a diminishing in the activity of the poltergeist.

She had a very clear reason for doing so – her father had been threatened with legal action if the ghost did not perform on cue. Janet Harper was again only caught out in the later phases of the visitation. Her frauds at this time were quite easily spotted. Furniture moving about in empty rooms was unconvincing, to say the least. It must be acknowledged, however, that some researchers felt that the Enfield case showed signs of fraud in the very early stages.

People do strange things, sometimes for the oddest of motives. There are cases on record in which people have made claims of ghosts and hauntings in order to be re-housed by their local council. Others have done so in order to frighten a relative whom they dislike. It is not entirely implausible that a person would seek to manufacture a poltergeist outbreak in their own home for such motives. Many of the more spectacular events

– those that would be impossible to fake – are witnessed by only one person, or at most only by the family concerned. When the six dining chairs in the Battersea Mystery House lined up like soldiers on parade and marched out of the dining room, the only person to witness the event was Mrs Perkins, a member of the affected family. The events that were witnessed by impartial outsiders, such as the policeman, would have been easier to fake. The lump of coal that hit the policeman on the back of the helmet could have been thrown by any member of the family acting as an accomplice to Mr Robinson. It seems unlikely, however, that families or individuals would seriously inconvenience themselves for frivolous reasons. The Robinsons suffered substantial financial loss because of smashed furniture, broken windows and lost rent when they were driven to move to another house. At the same time, it must be said that some people behave extremely oddly even when there are no supernatural forces at work.

People have sometimes persecuted neighbours to distraction for imagined slights. Newspapers often print stories about 'neighbours from hell' who play loud music, hack down hedges, swear and curse and generally make life intolerable for individuals against whom they have a grudge. So faking a poltergeist visitation in order to persecute a neighbour is not impossible. Looking at the Battersea case again, the idea that the neighbours were causing the damage was at first raised as a real possibility. This was entertained only during the early stages, when most activity took the form of coal being thrown about and windows smashing. Once furniture inside the house started dancing about, the idea had to be discarded.

So there can be no doubt that fakery and fraud are involved in some cases. However, other visitations have defied all attempts to discover any trickery. Most cases merely rest on the uncorroborated word of the families involved, but a few have been investigated by people of the highest reliability. On occasion they have witnessed things that they simply cannot explain. When Professor Lombroso watched wine bottles float through thin air at the Turin wine bar he was at a complete loss for an explanation. And then there was the policeman in the Ann Kidner case. He was impartial, sober and disinclined to imagine things but when he watched the loaf of bread levitate he was totally bemused. As soon as it stopped moving he inspected it thoroughly, but he was quite unable to discover what had caused it to float around. He arrested the hapless Kidner simply because he felt that she was somehow to blame. The lack of any evidence is demonstrated by her subsequent release.

All too often a sceptic will allege that an incident must be faked because otherwise it would not conform to the laws of physics. But just because something *seems* to be impossible does not mean that it *is* impossible. Until the late 19th century scientists did not believe peasants and farmers when they reported that large rocks sometimes fell from the sky. 'How did the rocks get there?' scoffed the scientists. 'Did a gust of wind lift a 20lb (9 kg) lump of rock up only to drop it on to the pigsty of an unsuspecting farmer?' The whole idea seemed impossible. Then somebody recognized that the lumps of rock were meteorites from space. Suddenly the impossible became not only possible but mundane.

Sceptics often suggest that a witness to poltergeist activity is mistaken. The idea has some merit. We have already seen that most of the families and individuals who report a poltergeist are living under conditions of stress. People who are distracted or upset are not the most reliable of witnesses, so some of the antics of a poltergeist could be explained in these terms. Mrs Wilkins, for instance, reported that she would often come home to find her daughter's bedclothes turned back, or toys moved about. It is at least possible that she had moved the toys herself and then forgotten about the fact. She may even have turned down the bedclothes when she was thinking about her daughter, without actually realizing she had done so. As for a poltergeist allegedly moving a bunch of keys from a hook to a table, most people have experienced this phenomenon. Forgetfulness and absent-mindedness are far more likely culprits.

However, the level of activity that surrounds some visitations is too intense for it to be blamed on forgetfulness. And while commonly used objects, such as keys, may be accidentally put in the wrong place it is more difficult to explain the movements of other objects. Consider the model duck that was repeatedly left in the middle of the floor, for instance.

It has also been suggested that apparent poltergeist visitations are caused by natural phenomena. For example, some houses in London are subjected to regular vibration strong enough to make pictures on the wall shudder noticeably.

There is nothing supernatural about this, it is simply underground trains passing by immediately underneath. Similarly, forces such as magnetism, static electricity and infrasound have been suggested as explanations for some manifestations. This might be the case, but the sceptics have been unable to reproduce the effects in laboratories.

Electrical devices are a favourite of the sceptics. Theories abound as to

*Out of nowhere: meteorites crashing to earth from the sky were reported several times by witnesses over the centuries, but were consistently dismissed by scientists as superstition until a rational explanation was found*

how lights can be switched on or off, how radios can malfunction – the list goes on. However, in the Rosenheim case several highly qualified technicians spent weeks investigating malfunctioning telephones and electrical systems. They could find nothing physically wrong. Indeed, they concluded that some energy not yet known to science was to blame. This natural phenomena argument also falls down when it meets the more spectacular exploits of poltergeists, such as dancing chairs and floating bottles of wine. It is impossible to account for chairs dancing around a room or bottles floating through the air. Hallucination might account for it – but not for the broken bottles and furniture that remain.

Finally, the most hardened sceptic must admit that a large number of poltergeist visitations have many features in common. So much so, that the possibility of fraud or error seems relatively remote. In fact, a researcher who is comparing accounts of visitations that occurred thousands of miles from each other and hundreds of years apart can easily confuse one with the other.

If the poltergeist phenomenon is genuine – and the weight of high-quality evidence would suggest that it is – then a solution must be sought. In past centuries the favoured explanation was that a hostile entity had entered the house and was causing the mischief. This entity might have been a ghost, a witch or a fairy of some kind, but it was generally believed to be intelligent, invisible and powerful. If one examines the reported phenomena, this solution has merit – provided that one is willing to accept the reality of such disembodied entities.

Many observers have likened poltergeist activity to having an invisible person in the room. Objects are moved just as if they are being carried by a human, except that there is nobody there. There is also the undeniable fact that many poltergeists exhibit both intelligence and personality. Those who are able to communicate do so with obvious intelligence. They respond to questions in a manner that is usually rational and logical – even if it is often untruthful. Even when direct communication is not established, the poltergeist seems to be aware of the people with whom it shares a house or a workplace. It will react to what they say and do. The Rosenheim poltergeist, for instance, did not move any paintings until Herr Adam commented on the fact and then it would not leave them alone.

Other poltergeists do not show such a high level of intelligence. The poltergeist at the mill at Appleby displayed enormous strength when it was shifting things about, but it did not have any obvious motive. It would stack boxes, smash windows and heave stones about, but it confined its actions to a single room and it never seemed to achieve a great deal. For all we know, though, it fulfilled some strange ambition of its own. It does seem very much as if the majority of poltergeists are distinct entities. But the case is not without its problems. If poltergeists were some disembodied entity that for some reason or another decided to take up residence in a house or office, it might be expected that they would come fully prepared to cause mischief. That is not the case.

Poltergeists do not suddenly arrive in a house with all of their future skills in place. They are not immediately able to talk, apport nuts, throw furniture about or perform any of the other spectacular manifestations. Instead, each poltergeist starts off slowly and builds up its repertoire of abilities over a period of time.

If poltergeists are demons or fairies, we can assume that each poltergeist is an entirely new demon that has never done anything similar before. This may be the case, but it seems unlikely. Having learned how to scare humans witless, a demon would surely seek to move on to the next house to enjoy its sport again. They do not seem to do so. In any case, suggesting that a disembodied spirit of some kind is the cause of poltergeist activity only complicates the situation. We know that there are humans involved because we can see them, but the existence of a demon, an angel or a fairy is entirely theoretical. There is no evidence for their existence other than the poltergeist activity. It would be much simpler and more straightforward to assume that the visitation was caused by the humans themselves.

If we examine poltergeist activity in those cases where the human background is fully known, the outbreaks make some kind of emotional sense. At Rosenheim the focus person did not enjoy her job and she resented her employer. It was the office equipment that was sabotaged, not the personal belongings of the other staff. And the constant telephone calls to the speaking clock suggest a desire to know what the time was. If the agent causing the events was the subconscious mind of the focus this makes sense. She would want to know the time, so that she knew how much longer she had to stay in the hated office. And she would want to damage the employer's property, but not the belongings of her fellow workers.

The case of the Wilkins poltergeist is also open to a more emotional explanation. Olive had recently married a wartime pilot at a fairly young age and had quickly fallen pregnant.

These circumstances must have made her yearn for the simpler, safer times when she had lived at home with her mother and father, who had cared for her needs as parents do. Whether it was Olive or Mrs Wilkins who was the focus, the emotional desire would have been the same – for Olive to be home, safe and snug. This would explain why Olive's bed was turned down, why her favourite toys were apparently played with and why her mother heard her come home so often.

Esther Cox went through the ordeal of an attempted rape. The poltergeist at first attacked her in physical terms and threatened to kill her. It then proceeded to act in a more disorganized and chaotic fashion, lashing out at anyone who got near.

This sort of emotional train is not unknown among rape victims. They first blame themselves for foolishly trusting a man, or for getting drunk in a nightclub; then they move on to become angry at the unfeeling world that does not seem to sympathize with their predicament. Again and again, the poltergeist seems to be lashing out in a purely emotional way, not in a logical way. It is not always possible to correlate the poltergeist's actions with the focus person and their problems. Sometimes it seems as if the person is *being* targeted rather than doing the targeting. It may well be that the focus is not the person with the emotional problems, but the one who is causing them. The emotional attack would then be centred on the person who was blamed for the problems.

This would suggest that the poltergeist phenomenon is unwittingly caused by a person who is unable to sort out their emotional problems by conventional means. Perhaps Anne-Marie Schneider was unable to get another job and so was stuck in Herr Adam's office. Virginia Campbell was certainly unable to move out of her cousin's bedroom. But that leaves the huge problem of how a person's subconscious mind can cause chairs to march around and stones to be thrown. And can somebody create a communication from an apparently intelligent entity?

This is where the Philip Experiment should be brought in. The evidence from that experiment, and those who have followed it, would indicate that people can cause physical effects by mind power. The Philip team discovered that the table knocking and other effects became less powerful if they were not all present. When one of the team members reminded his colleagues that they had invented Philip from nothing, the activity ceased for a couple of weeks. If the Philip Experiment, ongoing table-turning experiments and other studies are taken at face value it would seem that it is possible for humans to move objects using mind power alone. This process is called psycho-kinesis, or PK. Mainstream science does not recognize that PK exists. Consequently it is virtually impossible to find any reputable scientist willing to research it. It is even more difficult to find an institution that is willing to fund such research. But then there was a time when scientists did not believe that great rocks fell from the sky.

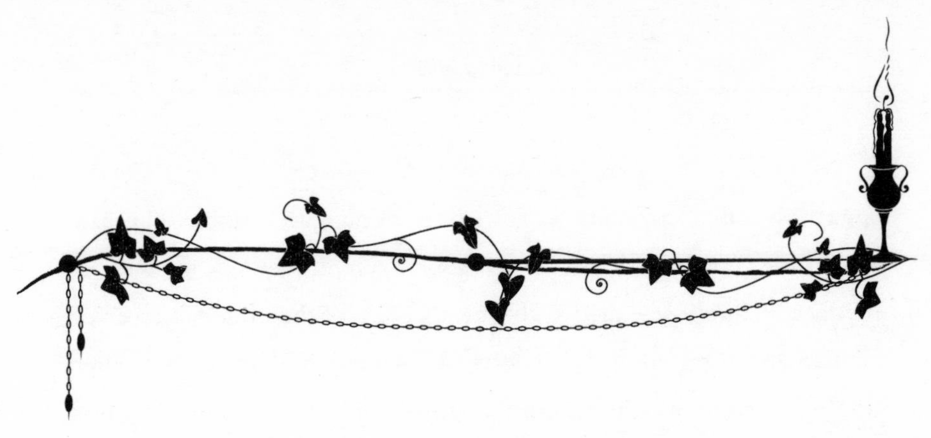

# afterword

# THE WAY FORWARD

Poltergeists are still active in the world today. Barely a month goes by without some local or regional newspaper reporting on a 'haunted house'. Just occasionally the outbreak reaches the national media, when it causes a brief sensation.

In August 2008 it was a house in Newcastle that received a poltergeist visitation. All the usual manifestations were present – stone-throwing, objects moving about, inexplicable thumps and bangs and even coins

appearing out of nowhere to fall to the floor with a tinkle. The case was made notable by the poltergeist's unprecedented mastery of modern technology – the family at the centre of the outbreak received abusive and threatening text messages on their mobile phones. Then text messages arrived from numbers that did not exist. The visitation lasted for ten months and then the manifestations trailed off. Normality returned to the house.

A rare note of levity was introduced by a poltergeist visitation at the Low Valley Arms in Wombwell, Yorkshire, in 2006. The lavatory in the ladies' cloakroom kept on flushing for no apparent reason. The baffled landlord first called in a plumber and then, suspecting an intruder, the police. When two policemen arrived they filed a report that confirmed the constant flushing and the fact that they could not come up with a rational explanation. Other manifestations followed. Barrels moved around the cellar, bottles were smashed, the fridge defrosted while it was switched on and the gas pressure inexplicably failed on several occasions. When the poltergeist was eventually contacted it claimed to be the spirit of an early 19th-century woman traveller who had been murdered by a man with a hoe on or near the site of the pub. This is a fairly typical claim for a poltergeist.

As with most cases, the formal authorities lost interest when they could not find a conventional explanation for these events. It was left to amateur investigators of the supernatural to take an interest. They told the recipients of the visitation what was going on and they recorded the manifestations. The investigators seem to have done a good, conscientious job. However, it would appear that no matter how much data is collected by amateur investigators there is a limit to how much they can achieve.

The media will continue to report poltergeist outbreaks as 'ghosts' or 'hauntings', even though the visitations are clearly something quite different. To be fair some newspaper reports recognize this fact, but it is usually buried deep in the text. While newspapers sensationalize the reports, scientists ignore them. The conventional view among scientists can be summarized as, 'it cannot happen, therefore it does not'. When challenged on any particular case, the response is that those reporting the event are either liars, or delusional, or stupid or some combination of all three. 'There will be some natural explanation,' I have been told on more than one occasion, 'you just haven't looked for it properly.' Coming from a scientist who has refused to even look at the evidence, still less look for a cause, this can be most infuriating.

But scientists are only human. They have their jobs to do, their families to care for and their gardens to till. It is perhaps too much to ask them to spend hours of their spare time searching for something that might not exist. And they also have their reputations to worry about. The academic world can be brutal and unforgiving. There are only so many professorships and research fellowships about. If an academic is seen to dabble with poltergeists his rivals might well take the opportunity to ease him out of his job and secure it for themselves.

What is needed is a respectable way for scientists to investigate the paranormal. That inevitably means conducting tests in laboratories. It seems that we must wait for the time when a poltergeist focus is willing to undergo tests and a scientist is willing to conduct them. But when will that happen?

*The burned-out ruins of Borey Rectory, which went up in flames after a lengthy poltergeist visitation reported in the 1920s and 1930s. Incidents included bell ringing, windows shattering, stone and bottle throwing, as well as wall writing*

# INDEX

# PICTURE CREDITS

Mary Evans: 22, 81, 86, 97, 99, 101

Shutterstock: 28

Clipart: 38, 49, 172, 254, 264

Bill Stoneham: 41, 53, 113, 155, 164, 174, 223

Shelley Revill: 66

Topfoto: 89, 151, 158, 170, 178, 187, 204, 207, 209, 214, 231

Linda Shaw: 131, 138, 197

Mark Dodds: 15